NOTHING
IN THE WAY

Clearing the Paths
to Success and Fulfilment

Kidest OM

Author of Consciousness of Health: Tuning into Absolute Well-Being

KIDEST OM

OTHER **BOOKS** FROM KIDEST OM

Anything You Want

Reality is a Buffet of Frequencies You Get to Sample

In Tune with Miracles: Cultivating Miracle Consciousness

Consciousness of Health: Tuning in to Absolute Well-Being

Vibrating Abundance: Creating Wealth from the Inside

Vibrational Weight Release

All of the above titles and more may be purchased by visiting www.infinite-life.com

ISBN-13: 978-1482685565

ISBN-10: 1482685566

For all Beings of past, present and future who have taken on, are taking on and will take on the work of self-growth, self-transformation, and self-transcendence. Thank you for re-writing the codes of our reality.

KIDEST OM

Contents

NOTHING IN THE WAY

Acknowledgements & Intent

I am eternally grateful to those who have in so many ways inspired, empowered, and propelled me into the perspectives I have moved into. No word can reach or encapsulate the freedoms I have found in my learning and in my growth. I have had and continue to have incredible teachers, mentors, and guiding lights who invite me to stretch my ideas and definitions of this experience, and as I have, I am only left with awe and gratitude for the blessings that await to be recognized and discovered by each and every person on the planet. I strongly feel that every individual, every extension and expression of the Creative Intelligence that births us, carries an unimaginable blessing inside themselves and that it is through the practice of self-awareness and self-transcendence that such blessings are unleashed into the world.

I am blessed with a supportive family, friends, and readers and listeners who forever fuel my creative escapades in the varied terrains of Consciousness. I am grateful for each and every person who has played their part in shaping me through their love, support, encouragement, and a life-long or short visit in my life. And I am grateful to this wondrous design for the moments that in every way leave me speechless.

My intent for this work is for it to serve as a solid platform of unparalleled expansion for whatever hopes and dreams are inside the heart and mind of each reader. I hope that it answers questions and plants curiosities that take you into more freedom, more fulfilment , and truer lasting success in the desired areas of your experience. I hope that these ideas, concepts, and invitations are not only catalysts but bridges that take you into new worlds of experience – worlds that clearly uphold and reflect the exact likeness of your free creative limitless self.

May all beings be inside peace.

May all beings be inside happiness.

May all beings be well.

May all beings be safe.

May all beings be free from the illusions of limitation.

Self Responsibility

The author/creator of this material does not, directly or indirectly, dispense medical or therapeutic advice or prescribe the use of any technique or Consciousness technology as a form of professional therapeutic treatment for physical, emotional, psychological, or medical conditions without the advice of an appropriately qualified health practitioner or physician. The intent of the author is only to offer information of a general nature. In the event you use any of the information in this material for yourself, which is your right, the author assumes no responsibility for your choices or actions. By using the material, you assume and accept full responsibility for any and all outcomes you experience.

"Arise, transcend thyself.

Thou art man and the whole nature of man

is to become more than himself"

- Sri Aurobindo

KIDEST OM

Introduction

Think about the success in your life or the things you consider yourself to be successful at. Most likely, when you ask yourself "what am I successful at" or "where have I succeeded in my life" you will look at the things and experiences that point to fulfilment and achievement. You will look at those areas in your life where you have been fulfilled or where you've achieved something you have set out to achieve.

Success, fulfilment, achievement, all point to the attainment of some desired end. These are principles of experience that operate in all spheres of life – in health, in relationships, in creativity, in personal development, in wealth and everywhere in between success and fulfilment can be achieved, can be experienced. Success in the garage working on the car, success in the kitchen creating some new dish, success in learning or developing a unique ability, success in the business world or the entertainment world, success in any endeavor makes use of the same internal mechanisms to different degrees of involvement. In all avenues of fulfilment and success your attention, your awareness, your internal organization, your psychology-energy-physiology are directly involved in the ultimate outcome of whatever it is you want to succeed in.

Your success in any endeavor, your fulfilment in any desired end, also ultimately ripples out to touch all other points of Consciousness, past, present, and future. Your success isn't really just about you, and it is not solely contained in the particular event you are aware of or focused on. Your fulfilment isn't really just about you. It may arise under the guise of self-progress, self-evolution, but ultimately that impulse is the impulse of the Universe moving through you. What lives you, what inspires you, what moves you, is a force and presence that is beyond the bounds of who you know yourself to be in any given moment. In an interconnected matrix of life, such as this one, there really is no single independent "I" nature that succeeds for the whole Universe organizes and cooperates in bringing about the desired outcome every step of the way.

The more you understand and are aware of the mechanisms through which you move into your desired end both individually and as the interconnected matrix of this experience, any desired end, the means through which you experience success, the more you can reliably perform and employ the mechanisms in new fields of experience. Consciously succeed in one desired end with all your eyes, including your third eye, your heart and mind open, and with your senses alert to the journey in the inner terrain's of Consciousness, and you will be able to repeat the performance in other fields of play that show up.

NOTHING IN THE WAY

What you will come to understand deeply as you move through this coded book – which isn't really a book but a journey through a field of Consciousness itself – is that the paths to success and fulfilment are first laid out and travelled in the inner spheres of awareness, in the inner terrains of Consciousness. Everything comes from within your being, first formed in the unseen realms of your inner worlds, in the deeper parts of your nature, and then expressed onto the canvas of your physical reality. The field of Consciousness is vast, and the hidden creative ground of all things. By this inner Field, all things are allowed, and by this inner world, all things are disallowed. Within this inner world rest dormant or unseen conditions for what can happen, how it can happen, how long it can stay or last, and so on. Seeds, patterns, blueprints, and templates source the conditions and events of all conscious experience – and the experience of success and fulfilment are not an exception to this outlaying of creativity from the inner realms of Consciousness to the outer fields of waking physical life.

What you must come to know and realize is that all conditionality, all conditions are first seeded in the mind and it is these conditions that come into activity the moment you set about to experience some desired outcome. Everything comes from within. Everything arises out of the inner realms of your own being. Just as the reality of your desired end in its completion lives as a pattern in

Consciousness, the reality of any obstacle lives as a pattern in Consciousness. Nothing is imposed upon you from some external source. Everything arises first in the inner realms of Deep Mind.

Clearing your path to success and fulfilment begins when you clear the mind with which you look outward. There really are no external conditions, only inner conditions being reflected and projected onto the screen space of experience. What you interpret as an obstacle and what you interpret as effortless are interpretations of a neutral environment created and sustained in the mindset you're using to observe your reality. Everything you see and observe and interact with is the embodiment of patterns of light and information you have aligned yourself to through your well-rehearsed beliefs and definitions about who you are, what your relationships are and what your world is. Your mindset precedes your interpretation of and interaction with reality. You see none other than your own mindset in the experiences you find yourself in.

It is when these mind-based conditions are loosened, neutralized or released that the path to success and fulfilment become clear, unobstructed. Beliefs are ways of organizing and coloring your perspective – they are conditions you impose upon your field of minded-ness to ensure you perceive reality within certain specified boundaries, certain specified hues. Out of these conditions, you develop layers upon layers of filters to allow yourself to distort information to fit your set and net of hues and conditions. You perceive none other than the terrains of your own matrix of mind. If you were to let go of your mindsets, you would find yourself operating in ways where you imagine, express and act without any reservation or inkling of impossibility.

If you can see the desired end and you can feel its reality in your mind's eye without any chatter or static noise interfering in the clarity of this inner seeing, then the unfolding of the desired end will be filled with ease and flow. For as long as there are obstructions and obstacles in the mind, in the form of low vibratory patterns of thinking and feeling, low vibratory image-making in the minds eye, however, they will appear on the pathway to success as events and circumstances to overcome or even as conditions that negate the reality of your success and fulfilment. By bearing witness to the activities within yourself vigilantly, you can come to know what you'll encounter in waking experience. If you go within yourself and clear these false limits first produced and sustained in the privacy of your own inner realm, the pathway to your success will be one of flow, synchronicity, and clear awareness.

Whatever you want to have in the world, you can have. Whatever you want to do in the world, you can do. Whatever you want to be in the world, you can be. All that you already see expressed in the world, you can express in your own life and so much more. Whether you resonate with this or not is a matter of what you have set up to be true in your own field of being, in your own spheres of awareness. Have you ever considered how you came to be aware of the rules of your reality? Have you ever thought about where you got the rules and the "how to's" of waking experience? Have you ever looked into why you have the definitions that you have about yourself? Have you ever examined why it is that you see and evaluate yourself as you do in the varied contexts of your experience, why you hold yourself high in some aspects of your life and low in others?

Whatever you think is possible, probable, likely in your mind will be just that for you, and whatever you think isn't possible in your mind will not be for you. It is only within your own mind that you create an opening to possibilities or you create limits for possibilities. You can expand your mind as big as the desired end you want to bring to pass and make that desired end reachable and containable – and you can contract your mind to be too small a space to contain that desired end and so make that desired end unreachable. It is the expansion and contraction of your own spheres of being that allow or disallow the desired outcomes of your waking world.

It is within your own mind that the rules to your fulfilment are set and so it is within your own mind they can be cleared. You can go against anything in the world and succeed if you do not have to go against yourself in the process.

David, meet Goliath, your very own self.

It is by your own mind that success is made and it is by your own mind that it is unmade. You and what you have calibrated yourself to is what is at play every step of the way.

Every individual already has within herself or himself the same inner mechanisms, inner forces, to bring about any desired end. The impersonal Universe does no favors, and it has no favorites. Every individual is equally equipped to achieve any desired thing. These inner forces are not limited to what you consciously know about who and what you are. They are greater, vaster, and limitless energies that are endlessly available to be sourced, to be accessed, to be utilized, to be leveraged in the formation of your waking experience.

The realization of any dream makes use of the same inner technology in everyone. And so success, fulfilment, the realization of any desire is much more about how you are doing you and how you are being you, than anything else you attribute these qualities of living to. And that understanding is what is offered here – an inner peek at how you do you as you move from one field of experience to another. The more you are aware of the mechanisms of change, of transformation, of transcendence, the more you can consciously utilize your multiple powers to bring about the change in landscape, both inner and outer, you so choose to bring about. There is nothing in the way – and your recognizing that will allow the natural materialization of the worlds you are dreaming of.

To make the best use of this field of Consciousness showing up as this book, bring to your mind an area in your life where you want to achieve or demonstrate some outcome. As you move through the chapters, the rooms of this expression, observe how the space and energy of what you are accessing apply in relation to you and this outcome you want to see manifested on your screen space. You can make the Consciousness available in these pages here as practical as you want by using the questions, prompts, and pointers to look at a specific outcome you want to step into.

Recognizing the Success Game

Everything in waking reality is a pattern of energy and information, of light, sound, and information behaving in specific and unique ways. Everything you see and don't see is a representation of Consciousness and a formation of Consciousness. From every angle you look at it, and at whatever level of inspection you examine it, it is a representation of Consciousness. There is actually no such thing as success outside of this game of waking reality and the illusion of being a separate independent self. In order to play the success game, there needs to be a "me" and an "other" of some kind – the "other" can be your environment, a situation, a circumstance, a relationship, a future version of yourself, anything that can be perceived as something apart and separate from you and from where you are right now. This is a beneficial point of awakening. Success and fulfilment are solely conceived and contained within the waking reality experience of separateness, independence, and other-ness.

Within this game is a starting point, an "I" frame of reference that desires or wants to move toward an endpoint, an "other" that is an event, outcome or achievement of some kind. There is a starting line, and there is a finish line, in between which is a journey of overcoming obstacles, gaining small and large achievements, and ultimately reaching the desired end. It is a hero's journey of sorts.

Success and fulfilment themselves, however, are not patterns you seek out to embody in sleep states like deep sleep, in meditation, or when the oscillation of the neurons in your brain are low or at rest. It is only when you are active in wakefulness and in the perception and sensation of being an "I" somebody, that you begin to think about ways of succeeding, ways of being fulfilled, or manifesting specific outcomes. You only ever create measurements of success when you are in fragmentary perception, in the motion of individuality and differentiation. In these perceptual states, you declare that having X, Y, and Z means that you are a success, while having A, B, or C means that you are not. It is within the field of having and being a separate identity existing in a world that is also separate and independent from you that the impulse to succeed and to be fulfilled arises. This isn't good or bad. And this isn't an expression that is here to talk you out of that game. It is a very fun game. It is just useful to recognize where the game of success takes place and what it involves. The whole game is entirely contained within your experiences of wakefulness and within your experiences of being a "me" inside a body who has desires of accomplishment. Beyond that, success, fulfilment, achievement are states, numberless unique oscillations of Consciousness, that hold no meaning or magnetism.

Recognizing the success game for what it is, a game you play specifically when you are operating within a certain level of wakefulness and within a certain sphere of self-reference, gives you the wiggle room and awareness you need not only to excel at playing it but to also play it with your own chosen rules. You can play the game as it is, you can re-write the code if you wish, or you can come up with your own pattern of success and fulfilment that takes this reality field by storm and becomes the new game. It really doesn't matter to anyone but you how you play the game and how you choose to show up in the game. So long as you recognize the game, you can play it any way you want. You can observe yourself as being inside it, you can observe yourself as being outside of it with a controller, or both or have other not yet define vantage points from which you look at and participate in the success game.

One of the central premises of this expression is that what you are, who you are, is beyond the confines of concepts, rules, and false boundaries superimposed upon an apparent you. You are not a limited "me" separate, isolated, and independent having to play a game all by your lonesome self. And while the tone and vocabulary of most mainstream ideas of how to be successful and fulfilled may not make use of your full identity, this expression does. If who and what you really are is the Undifferentiated Consciousness that is the beginning and end of it all, if who and what you really are is the creative convergence and unified expression of all of existence, then before you pop yourself into any arena to play, it is useful to you to recognize the waking reality games you are participating in from that expanded platform. Know yourself in your wholeness and then choose to bring into being whatever desired qualities you have selected from that perspective of your Total Being. The game you play from an expanded view of who you are is a different game than you would play from knowing yourself as a "me" inside a body.

The words success and fulfilment themselves are representations of patterns of Consciousness, ways in which Consciousness is sounding in the infinite flux of energy and information. Succeeding in a certain way in any given context involves a process by which information and intelligence get organized and re-organized to bring into visibility the end state. The entire process is a song, an oscillation of Consciousness with tones that shift and change as the pattern unfolds from one state in which the fulfilment is absent to the end state in which the fulfilment is present. Everything is sound. Everything is vibration. Everything is patterns within patterns of intelligent energy. And there are as many patterns for the experiences of success and fulfilment as there are points of Consciousness – infinite. Do you recognize how vast a playground you have to play in? Are you raising your eyebrow a little wondering just how much creative access and power you have and can have to play the success and fulfilment game?

Now having sparked this recognition of the success game in yourself, have you looked at the origin of your ideas of success and fulfilment? Where do your ideas of success and fulfilment come from? Where do your mental pictures of what success and fulfilment look like come from? Where do your experiences for what success and fulfilment feel like come from? Did you conceive of them? Did you adopt them from the world around you? Do you like, enjoy, and find excitement in your current conceptions of success and fulfilment? It's essential to recognize whether you are working with templates you've created out of the depths of your own unique creative expression or whether you are working from inherited ideas and blueprints of success, where the pattern of success and the rules of how they can come into being were not formed out of your field of Consciousness. You want to notice if you are writing the source code of your experience or if you are simply working off of someone else's codes.

Everything you know about success and fulfilment are command codes you make use of in executing your own experience of success and fulfilment. There are, in fact, no facts for how to be successful and fulfilled in waking reality. If matter is made up of mostly empty space, as modern science now states, then the hard facts of every facet of human experience are also primarily empty patterns. No fact or "how to" of any activity in waking life is actually really there – it is loose, with lots of holes in it, as mostly empty space. You want to tap into the flexibility of Consciousness that recognition offers you. There are suggestions, possibilities, tried and true mostly empty patterns being offered, executed, and perpetuated as the creative template out of which you form your own unique experience of success.

There are patterns upon patterns that are being utilized to create the experience of success and fulfilment. Yet these patterns upon patterns remain as but few selections in the Infinite Ocean of creative Consciousness. Success memes, success source codes, success blueprints abound in Consciousness like tools you can download from a website. These available and pervasive patterns, however, do not need to be the only ways in which you can flow in your experience. You have options. There are no limitations. There are no set formulas. There is only the perception of them. And perceptions are always malleable. Even what is offered you in this space right here, in this text, is but a dip in this Infinite creative ocean of Consciousness. So you always have at your disposal the ability to tweak, redefine, or altogether re-write the source codes and parameters of your experiences in the numberless Fields of waking reality. First notice where you are sourcing your ideas of success and fulfilment from, find out if they are codes you enjoy, and you can then build your unique experience of success and fulfilment consciously.

What if the experience of success and fulfilment could be filled with sustainable magic, recurring miracles, endless synchronicity, and limitless creative awe every step of the way?

Could your experiences of success and fulfilment in every single endeavor be filled, saturated, with such magic, awe and wonder? Is that a possibility? Is that a possibility that you are open to?

This is quite a different model from the mainstream model of hard-work, vigilance, sweat, and recurring defeat that later ends in triumph. But the journey to success and fulfilment can be as varied as the infinite points of Consciousness that are observing and consuming it. There are infinite windows and doorways, infinite angles and looking glasses to make use of. A journey of wonder and awe is no greater or lesser than a journey of heroic triumph, of meeting and overcoming obstacles. The question is more about what attracts you. What attracts one person to master the track and field, another to a swimming pool, and still another to a basketball court? There are many paths in wonderland, many different colored brick roads to walk along, and sparkling gold or emerald slippers along with the ruby ones to try on. Infinite possibility in experience and expression are the creative order of waking reality. So what you must look into and explore in any endeavor, in any form of your self-expression is, what you want that expression to be flavored by.

If you have unlimited options in your expressions of success and fulfilment, what do you want your unique experience and expression to be like?

What colors do you want it to be? If it was a piece of oil painting, with what colors would you paint it?

Give this some thought. Let yourself marinate in the idea of having innumerable ways of experiencing success. If you so choose, you can begin to infuse and lace your unfolding of success and fulfilment with magic, wonder, and awe by using these easy access codes:

If my experience of success and fulfilment were to be filled with sustainable magic, recurring miracles, endless synchronicity, and limitless creative awe every step of the way, how would it feel in my being?

NOTHING IN THE WAY

Access the space this offers you – let your every cell be encoded by the reflection that is extended to you from the answering Field as feeling.

If my experience of success and fulfilment were to right now be filled with sustainable magic, recurring miracles, endless synchronicity, and limitless creative awe every step of the way, what would I be noticing all around me?

If my experiences of success and fulfilment in every single endeavor were to right now be filled, saturated, with such magic, awe and wonder, what information would I be seeing, hearing, feeling, and coming into contact with?

Do you typically associate success and fulfilment with infinite probability, magic, miracles, synchronicity, awe, and wonder? If you look at and explore texts on success and fulfilment in the mainstream channels, you will usually not find magic, miracles, synchronicity, awe, and wonder amongst the endless descriptives used on how to be successful and fulfilled. You will find words like focus, concentration, drive, vigilance, failure, hard work, struggle, plan, realistic goals, willpower, and progress. Can you look at and feel the tones that are widely used, the colors that are most often infused into the expression of success and fulfilment?

Once again, each of these words, which are codes of light, can be very useful and can have their place in your unique expression of success and fulfilment. Yet you have to ask, is that all? In a vastly intelligent creative Universe that has with mathematical precision and exactness birthed unaccounted for star systems and trillions of intelligent species that we know of, is that really the only recipe for the experience of success and fulfilment available? Is success really and truly limited to the type of experience those mainstream concepts and constructs imply? And how easy or hard do you think it was for this living conscious Universe to have unfolded itself as it boundlessly has all around you?

Ponder that.

You get to choose the ingredients in your own unique recipe of success, the patterns you use to structure your experience of physical life. The concepts and constructs you accept as real around success and fulfilment are the commands you make use of to have and live your experiences of success. You author your energy, your psychology, your physiology and your relationship with your environment through your concepts, definitions and constructs. Your very electromagnetism, your ability to electrify and magnetize patterns in the Field, your ability to influence and repel patterns within the Ocean of Consciousness comes from those root codes you have integrated into your perceptual fields.

You can consciously participate in the formula and codes you make use of in the materialization of any experience. This participation begins with you first shining the light of your awareness upon the templates and blueprints you have integrated into your matrices of being. From that awakened awareness, you can choose to tweak those templates and blueprints, re-write them completely, or create new templates and blueprints altogether.

You have the choice, options, and support.

KIDEST OM

Question Your Assumptions

Sometimes moving into new fields of experience require that you turn your assumptions upside down, shake them around, and then turn them inside out before you hang them up to dry in the sun of your Consciousness. Does a journey of success and fulfilment need to have obstacles and challenges for it to be a worthwhile trip? What is an obstacle or a challenge and by what criteria do events become labelled as such? If you stopped interpreting your observation as being the observation of an obstacle or a challenge, what does the thing observed actually become? When what you're looking at is neither an obstacle nor a challenge, when such constructs are dropped from your psyche and vocabulary, what is it that you are looking at and interacting with? Are obstacles and challenges what make the journey satisfying? Is the landscape and scenery of the journey enough? If it's easy and effortless, is it still worth it? If it's easy to get, is it still satisfying?

These are questions worth rolling around in your mind so you can come into awareness of the rules and parameters you are on some level of Consciousness using. Typically, when you want to get something from the grocery store, you hop into your car and make that short drive, go in, pick it up, pay for it, and on your way back home you go. You rarely walk out of your home on such an easy mission with expectations of hardship, obstacles, and challenges. In your own mind, a trip to a grocery store is a mostly predictable and manageable unfolding. You start with knowing what you want and end with getting what you want with little to no friction or tension along the way.

Now you also have the option to set up this grocery store experience to be one of ease or one that's difficult. All the traffic lights you meet are green, there is very little traffic, and no line ups at checkout. You can decide to go to a grocery store that's an hour away, run into heavy traffic on the long drive, stand in line for 20 minutes or not even find the item you went to get.   The point here is that Consciousness can orchestrate and align with any version of any event – and this creative Consciousness is you. This creative power that can create and allow relaxed, flowing synchronistic moments is the same power that can create and allow a bumpy journey full of obstacles and triumph.

The experience of success and fulfilment is no exception. So you must ask yourself:

Are obstacles and challenges key ingredients in

my definitions of what a success journey entails?

Can learning and growth happen through curiosity, play, and exploration?

Can learning and growth unfold outside the duality of problems and solutions?

Are challenges necessary for the expansion of Consciousness?

Or can the expansion of Consciousness into fields of success be fluid, flexible, and relaxed? Would that be satisfying, exhilarating, and fulfilling?

If you ever look at young children or even domesticated animals, they play for the sake of playing. They explore for the sake of exploring. They study and observe things out of open curiosity. So is it possible to move into success and fulfilment through play, curiosity, and exploration?

You cannot believe in the validity of challenges, obstacles, and struggle and materialize a flow of events without them. Your belief in them necessitates their creation of them in your experience. Whatever you believe is true, valid, and necessary will show up. What you believe is the hard fact of waking reality will insert itself into your every experience. Even the great Houdini cannot escape the trap of his own concepts. Where concepts are, where constructs have been validated, is where boundaries of experience and to experience have been created. The truths you hold are open invitations you extend to patterns in the creative ocean to come and express in your personal reality. If in your model of waking life you believe that it is challenges, obstacles, and struggle that make you grow, then by your very assertions and insistence your reality will organize itself to give you the experience of growth in that way. Everything is an assumed fact, and assumed facts run rampant in the experience of physical life. When you hold such assumptions firmly to your heart, insisting on their validity and truth value, you are, in fact, allowing the expression of them in your reality matrix. The question is, do these specific illusory parameters of challenges and obstacles really interest you? And if they don't, are you willing to let go of your reliance on them? Are you willing to remove them from the stage of your conscious experience?

The facts of life, the facts of success, the facts of fulfilment are not actual solid facts the Universe is imposing on anyone. They are patterns of information, vibratory parameters, each individual sets for his or her own experience of waking life. You can change the assumptions and apparent rules at any time you so choose. The power of Consciousness is so vast and so limitless that you can do anything to any pattern including re-patterning the common mainstream ingredients of success. You can re-pattern an apparent obstacle into an open opportunity. You can re-pattern an apparent challenge into a direct source of tremendous power. Everything that arises in your journey has the potential to be turned into a great resource in complete service of your desired outcome. As you redefine your active principles of success, you redefine and remould the game of success itself. As you play the game you prefer to play, you reawaken yourself to the immense power that has always resided within you and expresses as you. In all levels of reality, in every sphere of Consciousness, you are actually unstoppable. You don't need to obliterate any boundaries or bust loose from any chains, you need only recognize that there aren't any boundaries or chains, to begin with.

The Fiction Game:

Here's a quick, entertaining game that will take you into your own pre-set limits around success and fulfilment. Write down everything you consider to be the facts of success and fulfilment. Everything. Leave nothing out. Get transparent and honest about what you believe success and fulfilment to be about. Think about each of the various life areas where success and fulfilment are an inevitable desire when mapping out your mindsets: health, fitness, family, friendships, love relationships, parenting, community, career, passion, personal development, creativity, spirituality.

Success in this area is...

Fulfilment in this area is...

In order to be successful in this area, I have to...

In order to be fulfilled in this area, I have to....

The ingredients of success in this area are...

The ingredients of fulfilment in this area are...

In order to succeed in _____ I need to ...

In order to be fulfilled in _____ I have to...

This list isn't about what you've heard others say or what you've read elsewhere about how to be successful and fulfilled. This is a list born of your own internal truths.

What is true for you?

What concepts and constructs are solid formed platforms inside of you?

Look within and answer truthfully to what you really think, feel, and believe it takes to be successful.

Are success and fulfilment your personal individual achievements?

Does a greater power, field, the Universe have a role?

Are you on your own or do you have support?

Are you a separate independent "me" on the journey of success?

Dig deep and bring as much of your concepts to the forefront of your awareness.

Once you have your list, draw a line through each statement of fact or truth you have identified.

Grab a colored pen and with each statement that's crossed out, write over it: FICTION!!!

Take a look again at your list. Did that hurt? Depending on the amount of significance you've given your current definitions a game like that or a process of that nature can be freeing, exhilarating, or disillusioning. No fretting though – you have complete choice in how you experience the undoing of your conceptual platforms. With every assumption or belief you uncover, you access and gain more energy for your intended and desired outcomes. That access to power, energy, and stability is available to you every step of the way. From the unravelling of patterns that don't serve you to the formation of patterns that do, you can feel the full force of the resources at your disposal.

All rules and all personal truths, all facts of any experience are made up. This isn't good or bad. And this isn't personal. Constructs upon constructs are what create the solid personal truths of every individual. Your world is formed out of the fabric of psychological constructs – patterns of sound that create concentric grids around your psyche, like a web a spider weaves. Within this recognition that it's all made up, is the flexibility of Consciousness that allows you to create new, more useful and supportive personal truths, new grids, and new blueprints. Such a change in your personal collected truths, or self-validated constructs, are what create new models of experience for each individual. You can have a direct conscious part in creating your models of the world, your models of waking reality. Your model of ongoing success and fulfilment can be one that exponentially builds and expands itself as it ripples out from your heart.

You Are Creative

The supporting structure of any event in your personal reality is you in consort with the interconnected matrix of creation. Your personal reality emerges from you, through you and unfolds as you. You are creative, a trait you inherited from the Prime Creative soundless sound that birthed you. To know yourself as anything or anyone is to create an intricate world that mirrors your knowledge down to the very last detail. Who do you know yourself to be as it relates to success and fulfilment?

Every event, including the experiences of success and fulfilment, come from knowing who you are and what you want, what fields of experience you belong in or want to belong in – and along with that is what structures of self you need to put in place to experience specific types of outcomes. Knowing where you want to go, what you want to plug into, and what you want to have plug into you is the starting point of every journey in Consciousness. It is what outlines the path or road to the destination. In a nutshell, it's a question of what it is that you really want, so you begin the creative journey by getting clear. What do you want? What you know and decide about what you want, will direct you to connect into the fields of resonance that contain the experiences and structures of self you desire. That first step of getting clear on what you want is like the co-ordinate you input into your Consciousness navigator, your internal positioning system (IPS). Your IPS will lock onto the coordinates of your destination and direct you there while also allowing you to download the information and patterns you need to integrate and fit right into that field of experience.

You gravitate toward and enter the fields you resonate with and match. You enter the circumstances and conditions that match your resonance. To resonate with something is to sway and wave in the same ways that it does – your oscillation of Consciousness, the waving of energy that you are aligns with and is in harmony with the energy waves of the thing you resonantly match. Everything you see about you and everything you will see about you corresponds to patterns, energetic structures that are active in the matrices of your Consciousness.

The way to activate the right patterns is to know with clarity what it is that you want, where it is that you are starting from and where it is that you want to end up. You can consciously choose to integrate into fields that reflect your preferred experiences of success and fulfilment. You can consciously choose to be attentive to the patterns, including awakening yourself to the expressions of individuals who reflect your preferred realities. Each one of these choices helps to shape the reality that you ultimately end up experiencing.

All that you know, all that you think, all that you feel and believe to be true is a spiral of vibrant creative energy you send out before you. Your path is always paved by the arrangement of your own heart, mind, and energy. The identities you hold are naturally creative. Your assumptions are naturally creative. You beliefs are naturally creative. Your feelings are naturally creative. Everything about you is organically and innately creative. Every decision you make, every choice you make, every excuse you make, every limit you imagine, every obstruction you say is there, honours your command – for what you assume is true for you is a command you extend in your field of experience. Everything, even the apparent obstacles, is an extension of who and what you know yourself to be and what you hold the world to be. You are continually translating aspects of yourself into the events and circumstances of your every moment.

Your innately creative nature means you have the power to bring about anything you desire, and you already do this on an ongoing and constant basis. Whether you are aware of it or not, all that you live is the materialized form of the desires you have entertained, entrained, and animated within yourself. You are creative, you are creativity, you are creative power. The world all around you is directly responsive to the desires you tell yourself are possible and to the desires you tell yourself are out of reach, unrealistic, or impossible. There are only cooperative components every which way you turn. What's visible to you and what you are visible to rests within the range of declarations you make about yourself and your world. Your personal affirmations, all the sounds you make, whether out loud or internally, are codes of light you use to arrange the creative matrix of waking reality. In the mutuality of Consciousness, whatever you can see, can see you. Whatever you cannot see, cannot see you. For it is your own calibrations of Being that reach and look back at you as your experiences, conditions, manifestations. You are creativity and creativity, is you.

Your world shuffles and reshuffles itself in response to your own conclusions. For as you are and as you know yourself, so your world appears and reflects. If you look out before you and decide to see obstacles, then the living Field in which you have your being will orchestrate and form itself into those obstacles. If you look out before you and choose to notice barriers and fences that keep you from what you desire to experience, then the world will reorganize itself to echo your choice of vision, your choice of seeing. If you look out onto your path and decide that your way is clear, your world will echo that seeing. What you experience is what you have selected and chosen to experience, consciously or unconsciously. It is never anything else. It is always your own body of beliefs and understanding that stretch out as your reality field.

NOTHING IN THE WAY

You are what you live.

Most often you unconsciously scatter your energy by imaging scenarios of why you can't, shouldn't, couldn't, wouldn't get what you want to experience. The moment a desire is noticed or felt to bubble up in your being, a 'yes' or 'no' is given to it. You either embrace it and see it as an inevitable reality or you reject it and conform yourself to the idea of its impossibility. In either scenario, you instantly begin making pictures, imagining, and dialoguing with yourself about this desire. Under the hood of your conscious awareness is an endless flow of activity that is in relationship with the broader creative Field. Even unconscious imagination is still creative. You energetically talk yourself into or out of your fulfilment constantly, and your reality conforms to that internal conversation.

Not succeeding in your desired end and succeeding in your desired end are equally creative acts that are persistently and continuously employing specific energetic mechanisms. You have to acknowledge the power of your creative self at every turn, regardless of how circumstances are appearing to turn out. If what you desire hasn't shown up, acknowledge yourself for the power you have in that. You are so creative that you will organize yourself to hide and be hidden from the thing you think you want. You're amazing. It's incredible. If what you desire has shown up, acknowledge yourself for the power you had in that.

Whatever the outcome, your creative energy has always been in play. You are always a plugged in participant in what you experience, whether or not that is consciously apparent to you.

When you know what you want, when you are clear on what you want, when you are decided on what you want, when your desire is clear, is precisely when you want to begin to pay attention to what creative mechanisms within yourself you are employing. This is when you want to look under the hood of your own creative vehicle. This is when you want to look inside at the thoughts coming to the surface, at the silent conversations you're engaging in within yourself, at the words you begin to speak in relation to the outcome, as the states of being you are moving yourself into either in support of or in contradiction to your desired end. You are either spinning yourself into the field of your desired end, or you are spinning yourself away from it. And you can become aware of which way you are spinning yourself as it relates to your desired outcome. Your creativity has no bounds and being aware of how you are doing you, how you are unfolding yourself will give you the leverage to fuel or support, and be fuelled or supported by the very fields of experience you are pulled toward.

The fields of experiences you are being pulled toward through your desires are as creative and conscious as you are, maybe even more so if you have not yet fully stepped into your creative power.

NOTHING IN THE WAY

Reality is a co-creation in the sense that what you create is also creating you, what you observe into being is also observing you into being. There is no separate independent self bringing something out of nothing. Every desire is the desire of a "we" for all who belong to some outcome have dreamt that outcome together. Nothing-ness is a living Field containing all realities, realities which are not static pictures but rather conscious intelligent systems with the same powers of creative observation inherent within you. That dream job has been dreaming of you just as you've been dreaming of it. That dream relationship has been dreaming you up just as you've been dreaming it up. These events you may from your current perspective, see as objects are not static objects. The event of a job or the event of a happy relationship is the creation of multiple points of Consciousness converging to bring about that reality. If you are dreaming of the ideal career, there is an organizational Consciousness dreaming of you, the ideal member of its evolving system. If you're dreaming of the ideal partner, the Consciousness of your ideal partner is dreaming you up in just the same way. Consciousness does not arise as an isolated incident, it is a whole dreaming, a multi-sided dreaming, where all parts are involved in the creative dance from the get-go, from before the desired event takes form in waking experience.

When you know what you want or what you desire, you want to then notice the relationship you are forming with this want or desire. If it's a healthy creative relationship, you will feel more alive, ignited, excited in the creative journey you have set into motion or that has established itself into motion through you. When it is a healthy relationship, you are in the awareness that what you want also wants you. When it's an unhealthy relationship you have formed with the desire, you will feel insecure, unstable, scattered, and even depleted. At this end of the creative continuum, you are aware of what you want, but you are splitting yourself and under the assumption that what you want does not want you. It's the drama of unrequited love you unconsciously play out with the desires you wish to experience. Whatever the quality, it is your own creative mechanisms that are being employed in the materialization or de-materialization of this desired end.

The beginning and end game of the whole journey is that it is all your creative expression. Out of the impressions within you, you birth the opportunities, avenues, and relationships that will take you into the levels of success and fulfilment that you desire. All boundaries, all lines, are superficial in nature and only contained within the definitions of your creative perception. When you look out into the world, the lines and edges you see with your senses don't actually exist in the finer and subtler dimensions of creation. It is your creativity that puts boundaries, barriers, obstacles in place. In Reality, there is nothing in your way.

NOTHING IN THE WAY

Do not go where the path may lead,

Go instead where there is no path

And leave a trail.

- Emerson-

The essence of true creativity is not to repeat and regurgitate what has already been said, done, demonstrated and expressed but rather to bring to life new possibilities of seeing, being, living while allowing the creative patterns already formed to evolve into new patterns. In a world that continues to hold that laws that are centuries old still apply to our modern world, such a notion of an ever-evolving creative matrix may be seen as fringe understanding. And yet nothing in the natural order of the Universe is what it was a fraction of a second ago. Everything is evolving itself beyond the confines of sameness and familiarity. A true creative exploit in any facet of human experience requires that you let go of going by, conforming to, the seeming rules, means, and paths that are said to be the way and the how of the world.

This absolutely also applies to the game of success and fulfilment as that too is a creative expression of your being. You have the option and the ability to create anew, new rules, new means, new ways, new platforms – untouched by the hands of familiarity and limitation, or at the very least you can modify and tweak the outdated century-old patterns of the game. The Universal ground of creativity is limitless, and you to your core are creative. As an extension of that boundless creativity, you are unbounded, free to draw from the ocean of infinite creative intelligence and bring your own unique expression of success and fulfilment onto the cosmic screen of waking life. To repeat, recreate, and perpetuate what's already been made visible in the world is really to perpetuate creative limitation, to stay in the same loop of limited observation. To demonstrate, or to materialize, from the vast ocean of the Unknown, on the other hand, is to demonstrate the godliness of your being.

Why remain fixed gazing at a small corner of a painting when whole galleries await your exploration?

To succumb to the practice of merely perpetuating the creative exploits of beings that have come before you – to take on the rules, ideas, assumptions that were left here for you unquestioningly is to cut yourself off from the limitless possibilities of expression that are always available to you. The rules, ideas that were left here for you are not valuable heirlooms. They are not the beginning and the end of what you can know, what you can be, what you can manifest in this world. We call those that go where there is no path pioneers, rule-breakers, and heroes and yet, that is the destiny of every heart and mind – to really blaze a unique trail of creativity in the world as an expression and extension of the Infinite.

Nothing that's been said is the final word.

Nothing that's been done is the only act.

Nothing that's been demonstrated is the only possibility.

Source from the Infinite Unknown and be Sourced by it also. Go into the Unfamiliar. There is no end in sight to the creative intelligence you can uniquely materialize in this realm of never-ending wonder. You can always choose to lean into the larger Unknown portions of Reality to glean and bring through versions of success and fulfilment never before seen in the world. You have that option. You have a never-ending buffet of options.

KIDEST OM

Things Don't Just Happen

Physical focus and being solely focused on the external world the senses present may make it seem like things are just happening left right and centre, that you have no part to play in what arises, in what moves toward you and in what leaves your experience. When the mind is focused and fixated on external reality, this perception and perspective that everything is happening all by itself can be a believed and lived experience. This limited idea that things just happen by chance or accident is born of the mind of separation. You exclude yourself from the process of creation, from the Universe, from the creative process and flow of existing, as though you are someone who is apart and external to the flow of the vast living Universe. You hold yourself separate from a world that seems to carry on all around you. You exclude yourself from the flow of life, and you fail to see that you are a part of the unfolding, a very much integrated and interlinked participant in the dance. Things don't just happen. Nothing comes into being by chance or accident or as an event that is separate and disconnected from you.

From such a dis-jointed point of reference, you hold that things are happening to you through some unknown and unpredictable manner or power. Or at the very most, you attribute an external force or power to be doing things to you and for you, through once again some unknown and unpredictable law or command. Within such a reference point, at every point of experience, you exclude yourself from the creative process and hold your life and experiences to be in the hands of something "other" than yourself. "Things are happening to me," you say silently to yourself. "Things aren't happening to me," you say quietly in the privacy of your own mind. The states of being this reference point gives you access to falls on a broad spectrum of insecurity, while even in the most devout commitment to some external power, you still find yourself in mindsets of doubt, mistrust, discord, confusion, and disharmony.

For as long as you hold yourself in the perception of separation, division, or fragmentation, that practice of holding yourself external and seeing yourself as the recipient of uncertain events, you keep yourself blind to the participatory nature of your being within every moment in which you find yourself. Nothing just happens to you. Nothing is by chance or accident. And nothing is forced upon you by some external or greater power. Everything that forms you've had a hand in shaping. Everything that arises, you have had direct input upon. When the mind that was previously exclusively focused on the external turns inward toward the interior space of thoughts, beliefs and your well-rehearsed stories about yourself, others and your world, this realization that you have a hand in all that you live and in all that lives you is clear as a sunny day.

NOTHING IN THE WAY

Holding yourself outside of the creative flow of your experiences keeps you in the slow spinning state of dis-empowerment when, in reality, you have always been a participating agent in the flow of your experiences.

You have a direct hand in everything that comes to pass – whether consciously or unconsciously you participate in the manifestations of all patterns in all parts of your experience. Nothing, whether desired or thought undesired, is forced or imposed upon you because nothing can be. Patterns of experiences do not come to you or happen to you, they happen through you – everything flows into being through you as its entry point into your lived experience. You are the intersection point of creation, where the unseen comes through to be the seen, where the invisible moves through to become visible. The spectrum of all wanted, and unwanted circumstances flow into form through every point of Consciousness, every entry point of creative intelligence – and those entry points are all intelligent living systems that Consciousness makes use of to bring about the experience of physical reality. This entry point and this flow of intelligence are both you.

Moving or awakening into the power of conscious manifestation requires that you eliminate any notion of such self-exclusion, of being an effect or being at the mercy of some disconnected external power. You cannot hold yourself to be an effect in your world. You cannot hold yourself to be a powerless spectator in your experience. You cannot hold yourself in a state of no-power inside of this Universe, for in that stance you give up the chance to consciously witness the very creative miracle that you are.

Through the very thoughts you think, through the very beliefs and expectations you habituate, through the very states of resonance you hold yourself in, you are directly participating in the world that forms around you, and in every single event that constructs itself in front of you. You are right now contributing yourself, your resonance, your flow, your focus into the Creative Field of life. This self-contribution will create the echo that you will experience as the circumstances and conditions of your personal world. Whether you are conscious of it or not, you are directly plugged into, contributing to and in relationship with whatever patterns manifest themselves as the events and conditions of your life. Every event that has come about in your life has been one that was mobilized, fuelled, and fed by you.

Nothing comes out of the blue if you are attentive enough to your own inner spaces of being. You will see the very means by which you mobilize and fuel patterns until they become solid appearances on the screen space of your experience. Any area of your life where you don't own the power you have within it in this way is an area in which you are squandering your creative power. The beginning of your understanding of the creative power that is available to you is taking ownership of all that you have experienced. Know that all you desire to experience is also in that field of ownership. Claiming your power, owning your creative power, taking the seat of your creative authorship begins by your looking about your world and awakening to the realization that all of it is your creative expression. All that you are living is the externalization of who you have known yourself to be, and who you right now know yourself to be. In that recognition alone rests the power of many worlds. What sees and awakens in this seeing as you look out with such ownership is the vast Universe itself.

Awaken yourself to the creative power you have in your experiences, in your moments. Awaken yourself to the power of your attention, focus, awareness, and heart. Awaken yourself to the power of the identities you steadfastly hold. Awaken yourself to the boundless Field of intelligence you are continually drawing from to bring about the world, whether liked or not, you have formed around you. Begin in this awakening and start to notice what awareness starts to come alive in you, what begins to recognize itself as this you.

A greater organization or order of being does not originate out of complacency, heredity, unconsciousness, or chance. The way your nervous system is calibrated, what you are attuned to and harmonized with is not left up to unknown or uncertain factors or forces. The art of self-structuring, self-organization, ordering your being to be attuned to desired realities is your own creative responsibility. As you have the ability to stretch your parameters, as you have the ability to alter your dominant states of being, as you have the ability to cast your awareness and attention into any field of experience you desire, you are ultimately equipped with all that you need to move into the experiential spaces you prefer. As you take hold of this power, a greater unseen power takes hold of you.

Nothing is hidden, and nothing is withheld. What has already been demonstrated in your world, all that you right now think is miraculous or unheard of, all that you see with disbelief, is not even the tip of the creative iceberg. The capacity within every field of potential expression in Consciousness is infinite. It is limitless. There is no cap but the cap put in place by the restrictions of learned rules, manufactured definitions, and expectations. If you could let go of all of your expectations for what can happen in your personal world right now, if you could just drop all parameters of "this is how things are", how much room opens up? This ability you have to access the boundless, to move your attention over and through illusory boundaries, and embody the boundless is itself an ability of infinite depth. There is no end to how open you can become. There is no end to how receptive you can be. There is no end to how much integration of more flexibility in Consciousness you can allow for yourself.

The premise that you are where you are, that things just happen, and that "this is it" is one that creates false limits on your own capacities to expand into the Infinite and the boundless. This isn't It. This will never be just It. Look through the surface appearance of whatever has shown up around you and reach into the limitless power and resource it carries within it. All that you see is meaningless and yet at the same time contains immense valuable power within it. All that appears can actually further source your growth and advancement in any desired direction whether you want to move deeper into the inner spaces of your own being or extend more out onto the projected space of waking life. It takes your recognizing the potential contained there to make use of it.

No-thing just happens.

KIDEST OM

Consciousness Does Not Fail

The fabric and substance of both matter and the immaterial is Consciousness. It is the force, the power, and the animation of all of creation, and it is the One force, substance, and power that appears and gives the illusion of plurality to the material world. Consciousness pervades all and is all – it is the intelligent and aware atmospheric presence in which all things are. It is Consciousness that exists as the potential of everything and the potential in everything. Greater than what can be perceived, vaster than what can be reached, deeper than what can be plunged into, is Consciousness. It is this Consciousness, the true nature and identity of all things, that does not and cannot fail – for you can never fail to be who and what you have always been, you really are, and will always be.

Consciousness both forms and transcends all boundaries, all perceptual limits. It can move through and dissolve any apparent barrier, and it can move or arise to appear as any evident barrier. Boundaries can be seen through, for what seem to be boundaries are themselves Consciousness. Limits can be moved through, for what looks like all limitation is itself Consciousness. Consciousness extends and expands itself in all directions of experience, arranging itself into endless patterns within patterns, and as It does it gains more awareness to bring all patterns into its light. Everything around you and within you is a different and unique ordering of Consciousness. From the atom to the molecule to the cell to the human organism to the earth organism to the cosmic organism, on all planes and at all levels Consciousness organizes itself into clusters of intelligence. At all levels and on all planes Consciousness uses the same mechanisms to know and unfold itself. The journey of Consciousness and the journey within Consciousness is always one of self-recognition.

If you can right now extend all aspects of yourself into the threshold of the limitless, where there is no threshold, and move this extended and expanded awareness through all areas of your experience, what do you notice?

How far, how wide, how deep can you stretch when there are no boundaries to hold you?

Consciousness does not fail. You are continually demonstrating this primary principle by what forms around you as your physical reality. The resonance you have achieved and sustained never fails to bring about matching realities. Every single manifestation, every single moment, every single detail of your waking world is the brilliance of Consciousness being displayed. You are now succeeding in the way you've aligned yourself to succeed, whether that success is in the absence or presence of some experience. You are succeeding in experiencing a reality of not having what you desire in the same way you are succeeding in experiencing a reality of having what you desire. You are now being fulfilled in the way you've aligned yourself for fulfilment. You're fulfilled in the dream of now having what you want and you are fulfilled in the dream of not having what you want. Both absence and presence, both the lack of and the having of some end are creative expressions. You organize reality to hide the desired end, and you organize reality to reveal the desired end. The absence of some outcome in some area of experience is precisely as you have internally organized it to be – you are succeeding in creating the experience of the absence of your desired outcome just as you are succeeding in creating the experience of those things that are fulfilling and elevating you. Consciousness has never failed to bring about innumerable qualities of experience.

Consciousness arises as desire, and then Consciousness extends itself as the fulfilment of that desire or as the resistance to that desire – either outcome is the success of Consciousness forming itself into the material world. The way events organize, the way situations arise, the way moments assemble themselves all around you, are all unique demonstrations of how unfailing Consciousness is in its creative pursuits. This is what you are and this is what you are made of in each and every moment. The fabric of your entire being is this unfathomable creative something that raises itself out of apparent Nothing.

Manifestation, all manifestation, is Consciousness in action – it is the states of Consciousness being acted out by form, by matter. The apparent presence of a desired outcome or experience and the apparent absence of a desired outcome or experience are both manifestations. You are manifesting the reality of having what you desire just as you are manifesting the reality of not having what you desire. Either end of the continuum is a creative act, an expression of Consciousness in which the landscape of waking reality is organized to fulfil the maps of possibility held within your being. It is Consciousness dancing and twirling its creative skirt in the play of physical experience – Consciousness is the stage, the props, the story, the players, directors and the audience. The circumstances that gather, the conditions that form, the relationships that arise are all the bodies of the energetic resonance you have maintained yourself in. Infinite creative success is all that is at work in every single moment, whether wanted or unwanted by the self you take yourself to be. What looks like success and what looks like failure equally employ the technologies of Consciousness to come into form.

NOTHING IN THE WAY

The avenues and channels of Consciousness are endless. Consciousness continuously and creatively manifests itself into matter, circumstance, condition, and relationship. There is an unwavering certainty in the ways Consciousness forms itself into the contents of waking reality. It's unconditional, certain, solid, unquestioningly convincing. You can't have it? No problem, Consciousness will convincingly demonstrate that. You shouldn't go there? No problem. Consciousness will convincingly demonstrate that too. It's all yours? Fantastic. Consciousness will put on a very intricate and elaborate display to confirm, that yes, indeed it is all yours. Whatever parameters are set and have been set, Consciousness will fill and color it and demonstrate it in ways that will floor your conscious mind over and over again. How many times in your life have you said "I can't believe this happened to me" whether in the context of some desired end or undesired end? That is the creative wonder of Consciousness at work.

Circumstances are the mirror through which you notice what you have declared in Consciousness. Consciousness decides, whether through certainty or doubt, whether through choosing or not choosing, whether through accepting or rejecting, and these decisions are reflected in the conditions that form in waking experience. Take away the superficial label of success and failure and what you have is the varied expressions of Consciousness in form.

KIDEST OM

Consciousness is the beginning, the middle, and the end. It does not fail. Remove the very notion, construct, the bounded sound of "failure" from your vocabulary. There is no usefulness to it when you are working from the solid ground of who and what you really are.

Seeing Infinite Possibilities

Your physical eyes, your physical senses, only show you about less than one percent of the whole of reality. Less than one percent. Your mind only shows you its biased and filtered representations of the past. What appears and what you habitually expect to experience in your life is based on a limited and limiting lens of memory and massively partial sensory data. So to go by appearances, to go by what appears to your sense instruments right now, is to limit yourself to less than one percent of what's really available to you. To go by your memory is to restrict yourself to inadequate representations of what's truly possible in this moment. There is so much more available to you right here and right now than the visible world and your memories can show. Let yourself rest inside of that recognition for a moment. Take a long deep breath and sit inside of that. What possibilities rest awaiting your attention right now in the 99.9% of the reality field you don't see? What's truly present and available for you to access beyond the images stored in your mind? How many fields are here? What is alive and prepared for you in all of what you don't see right now?

What appears right now is already changing. What appears right now is not rock-solid. What appears right now is a fast moving showcase of light and information – a vibratory field that is in a constant state of flux. What appears right now is already fading. The face of constant change is what you're looking at all around you. What appears right now isn't it. And it isn't it right now. Or right now. It's already changing and has changed in uncountable degrees from the moment you started reading the first paragraph of this page. Change is rapid. Change is fast and constant in the phenomenal world of waking life. Change is the norm, the baseline, the starting point.

Sameness, solidity, fixed-ness, continuity are mechanisms you employ to create the experience of a stable reality. A permanent reality that makes sense to the conscious mind and to the self-narrative of being a continuous "me" having an ongoing experience. Your autobiographical memory relies on continuity, for things to be the same now as they were a moment ago. The sense of having a stable identity, a stable point of reference is based on this projected continuity where things don't change, and if they do they only change a little bit within the boundaries of what's comfortable to your sense of self. The tendency of the nervous system to average out and "normalize" information so that it's within the range of acceptable experience, comfortable and familiar experience, an experience that is in accord with your rule-sets and belief parameters is one that keeps you from experiencing just how fast-changing "physical" reality really is. If you picked up a book and it had no logical sequence to follow or a story that was consistent, you'd drop it confused and altered by its un-dependability. So you create a sense of dependability out of the infinite flux of energy and information to weave a storyline, and hopefully, one that you are enjoying. You do this by continually filtering out data that contradicts your truths and by regularly putting the past in front of yourself. You take your stored images and put them in front of yourself in your mind's eye, and you expect that image to be what you encounter in the next moment and the one after that. You do this so effortlessly and habitually that to you, linear flow of predictable events and experiences is assumed to be just how things are and just how life happens. Still, it remains that all that you see before you and all that you don't see are patterns upon infinite patterns you are using to form your experience of waking life.

Look past all appearances, all that has already formed. You have the ability to do this, to pierce through the veil of apparent solidity and into the 99.9% of infinite possibility that surrounds you. What don't you see right now? What is here and beyond your sense instruments right now? What's here for you to rotate your awareness toward? What's living and in communion with you within the space that surrounds you? Give that your full undivided attention. Leave all the sensory data alone for just a moment. Stamp a "draft" watermark on your perceivable world right now, on all that is visible to you. All the data you see and take in with your senses, all the details visible to you as your current reality and environment is a very tiny spec of information you have assumed to be your total reality. What don't you see all around you? With your mind's eye and your hearts antenna you can explore the invisible, the unseen, the seemingly not yet formed which is actually the Field that you are always immersed in. As an intersection point between the unseen and the seen, you are immersed in both the invisible and the visible. You have an all-access pass, an ideal position in the creative expanse of this living Universe. You can let yourself be guided by curiosity into the unseen terrains of the invisible whole. You can go past the world you see and look right into the expansive ocean of infinite potential in which you are immersed every which way you can turn. You can sit face to face with Infinity in every moment.

Everything you can imagine and everything you can't even begin to conceive of is here right now pervading the very space that seems to hold in place your visible less-than-one-percent-of-the-whole-picture reality. You can look through any manifestation and notice that there is infinitely more for you to experience. There's always infinitely more to experience right on the ground you stand on, on the chair you sit on, in the room you are in. You can treat every appearance as a portal into the Infinite, everything as a doorway into the exponential More-ness that forever remains hidden from sensory experience. This is always going to be the case. There is always going to be exponentially more available to you than what's currently appearing before you. No matter what has come into view and how much of it has come into view, there is always more. There is always going to be more for you than what you're looking at as your current reality.

Whatever has formed, whatever has manifested is always going to be less than one percent of what's possible for you, what's prepared for you, what's awaiting you. This is the nature of Infinite access. It just never ends and can never end. Think about that for a moment. Infinity means no end. Limitlessness means no boundaries. This is what you have your being inside of, and this is what is inside of you.

When you recognize this, your movements become about surrendering yourself to the Limitless. You let yourself become Still, you move out of the realms of what's known in your world, the realms of what has already manifested, and dissolve yourself in the field of the Infinite, the Unknown, the not yet born. In the states of least observable motion in Consciousness, you stand expanded as the Field of limitless possibility itself. This is the evidence of real maturity in your perception. When you know that the Unknown blesses you infinitely more than you can imagine, you willingly let go of your rules and conditions to be an opening for this invisible source and resource of endless possibilities. Be Still and know what you can never put into concepts. Be Still and touch the body of pure Grace. Be Still and let yourself be the Still center of Creation.

The state of not knowing actually gives you access to unbounded freedom. You can leverage this. Whatever you are experiencing and whatever you want to be experiencing, when you recognize that you actually don't know, you angle yourself differently to know it. The known and the Unknown always work together to change, modify, or bring into being a new pattern of experience. You can use this "know/don't know" state of wholeness to move into the reception of whatever you desire.

Access balance by using these codes where ever you need to bring yourself to the middle of both knowing and not knowing:

I don't know how this will come to pass, but I'm excited to find out.

I don't know how my desire is fulfilled, but I know that it is.

I don't know how life blesses me right where I am, but I know that it does.

NOTHING IN THE WAY

I don't know what I don't know, and I know there is a part of me that knows all.

Points of focus like this re-tune you to the field of endless blessings, to the realm of infinite possibilities, that permeate all space and all time and all that is beyond. You can at any point, bring yourself into resonance with not knowing the means and the way, but knowing that they are there intelligently designed and orchestrated by the creative forces of this living Universe. You can know and not know simultaneously, and in that middle way find much freedom to access, receive, and make use of the streams of information and guidance that are always flowing to you and through you.

You are always drawing energy from the continuum of the personal to the Infinite. You are either drawing from your personal field, exerting will and focus, or you are drawing from the Universal flow of Infinite Possibilities. In the latter, you are moving through your world as an opening to the Unknown rather than a point of origin of the known. What you accomplish through personal will draws on your own reservoirs of energy and power. This is what you work from when you think you know the means and the way, when you think you've figured out how it's going to happen, when you assume you are the one that's going to make it all happen. You are working from your perceived circumference of energy, your perceived personal field as an independent and separate self. This is neither good nor bad. No process or way of referencing and materializing is good or bad. Recognizing where on the continuum of flow you are sourcing from, however, will allow you to make the necessary calibrations of self to have the best possible experience you can have. Your energy is creative regardless of from what level of being you extend and express it. You can remain in that awareness of separation and still create a beautiful life. You can also expand that circumference, widen and extend it to include more identities, whether group, cosmic or nonlocal and experience a different way of living. You can be a single "me", and you can be a connected "me", you can go beyond this "me" to express a different quality of being-ness. It's all allowed, and it's all creative. Consciousness will be creative in any order and at any level of self-perception.

When you operate from the Universal flow of Infinite Possibilities, going beyond your personal and personalized energy field, you open yourself up to both known and unknown channels of fulfilment. You open up to the support of unseen forces that span into realms invisible to your conscious mind. You draw from a limitless reservoir of energy, inspiration, creativity, insight, and so much more. Your movements become guided by more profound energies, broader seeing, and timeless principles that move into play as you move your limited sense of doer-ship out of the way. In seeing Infinite Possibilities, you open yourself up to infinite resources that move you into infinite channels of success. When you move into the Infinite, when you expand your parameters of self or even erase them altogether, the unobstructed Infinite moves through you and as you. Whatever level of inclusivity you allow for your being will serve the journey you embark on.

Anytime you engage in the process of creativity, the conscious mind and the intellect formed of the known will chime in. Control comes into the equation and you find yourself trying to juggle the unknown aspects of what's taking shape. What you will often experience in that is tension, frustration, or even confusion as you try to grasp at and arrange what hasn't come into full form. This is where you must give up your conscious ideas of what can happen and how it should happen to the greater knowings and unified seeing of intelligent Universal Flow. This is really a Flow you are at one with always. It isn't that there is a separate flow called your own individual flow and another called Universal Flow – what these distinctions point to are the boundaries you draw in your perceptual reference points. It is Consciousness that contracts into an apparent separate and independent self and it is this same Consciousness that expands and realizes itself as the Universal. Still, the distinctions are useful in pointing out the boundaries of being you may be drawing or erasing for yourself. This, once again, comes back to you knowing how you are doing you.

Initially, what aspect you are in service of takes conscious noticing on your part. Are you in service of your conscious limits or are you in service of an expanded flow of intelligence and design? The very states you experience moment after moment will indicate to you whether you are in the seeing of Infinite Possibility or whether you are in the limitation of conscious knowing and doing. Notice where you are sourcing from in your experience. If you are sourcing from a sense of a limited self in a body, independent and separate, you will know it by the level of tension you experience. When Consciousness contracts into the sense of a separate self-nature, that is reflected in a level of tension that ranges from subtle to outright uncomfortable. If you are sourcing from a field that has no point of origin, that has no location, you will experience a freedom of movement in your experience.

The assumption that you have to be involved and mentally in control of the unfolding of the bigger things you desire in your experience silently negates that greater intelligence that is unfolding all parts of the Universe right now. Whatever has organized the body's intelligence, whatever has organized the spin of the planets, whatever has organized the trajectory of the sun, is and has always been at work at all levels of reality, including the games of success and fulfilment being played in your waking world. This isn't to deny the intelligence of your own conscious being but rather to include the whole aspect of intelligence you are not in conscious perception of. Include the Field of Infinite Possibilities, include the presence of Universal Intelligence, include the awareness of a greater hand at work in the orchestration of your moments, and you will release yourself to expand and flow with this greater flow rather than remain contracted, likely moving yourself spastically within it. But maybe sometimes it's fun to splash around frantically in the creative ocean and pretend you aren't one with it?

What has manifested is just that – it is manifestation, no matter how grand or appealing the form, keep your gaze locked on the Infinite. Be unwavering about this. If you become distracted by the manifested world, if you again become absorbed in outer reality to the exclusion of the deep inner terrains of being, the spastic frantic splashing around will once again be your reality. Attention and awareness, energy and information, are directed differently through the nervous system when attention is fixed or more oriented toward the Non-local. In your awareness of the Infinite, there is no boundary or line or location to latch onto. There is space, boundlessness, a field that has no beginning or end. Depending on the manifested is like settling to live from a cup of water for the rest of your life, even though you have an entire natural spring water source in your backyard. Manifestation, what has already formed, paths and means already in view, what has already come into view, what has already materialized is on the surface always finite, limited, bounded. It is not a source of new information, inspiration, or movement, at least not on the surface. You want to let it go and fade and remain attentive to the broader, greater, creative Field.

There is always more to be noticed than what has already come to pass. Something desired comes to pass and you turn your attention away from the limitless field that sources your world and onto the finite form it has formed itself into. You can celebrate, acknowledge, and appreciate what manifests while still keeping your sight on the Infinite Possibilities that are still pulsing, living vibrations all around you. There is always more underway, on its way, being shaped right now even as you appreciate and give thanks to your current blessings. This is the way of Infinite Possibilities, the flowing current of endless blessings.

What would it be like if you gave your undivided attention to the field of Infinite Possibility right now?

If you were to right now rely entirely on the blessed flow of the Miraculous Unknown, what would you stop holding on to?

How does it feel to be sourced and resourced by

*this Infinite Field in every area of your
experience?*

Your reality has the potential to ignite a sense
of awe and wonder within you every step of the
way. The experience of that, the living of that, really
begins when you open up to the unseen
possibilities of your world and self. Are you open to
the possibility of experiencing your success journey
in a way that allows you to realize just how vast a
miraculous field the world about you really is?

KIDEST OM

Success Energetics

Success does not manifest by chance or accident. It cannot. Nothing in this reality is by chance or accident. Success in any endeavor is the outcome of full graceful multidimensional alignment between heart, mind, and biology or Consciousness, psychology, and physiology. Within these three realms are endless forces that synchronize and move into place to create the harmony, resonance, and coherence needed for some desired end, some field of success to materialize and stabilize in your waking world. There is actually so much that collaborates, coordinates, and cooperates behind the scenes to bring about any state of alignment and any experience of fulfilment. Most often such a process of alignment occurs beyond the realm of conscious awareness, and yet if you listen enough and are attentive enough you can tune into and become aware of the gears that change as they change in your movement toward and into some desired field of fulfilment.

You can enter the hidden elaborate dimensions of your being to access greater awareness on how to move and organize yourself so that your preferred realities are best supported and fueled into being. Beyond the curtain of conscious awareness is a greater awareness, your own, that is entirely and continuously alert to the mechanisms of change and transformation. Just as there is a greater awareness that is attuned to every minute step of the caterpillar's journey and transformation into a butterfly, there is this same awareness that is alert to every shift and sway of your being as you move from one field of experience into another. You can tap into and leverage this awareness to learn what the most resourceful and optimal states of being are for the experience of ongoing success and fulfilment in your personal reality. There is such deep abiding magic to everything about you, that when you really look at how you work, you can't help but be in awe of the intelligence that forms itself as every layer of your being and every pixel of your waking reality field.

States of success have their own posture, their own presence, their own configurations psychologically, emotionally, biologically. A state that supports the experience of success, for instance, is a state that moves you into a more confident space of being – you present and call forth from a different level of consciousness, awareness, and presence. Move yourself into a state of confidence for a moment and notice what that feels like. Think of an area in your life where you have total confidence in yourself, in your ability, in your capacity – where you feel and know that you can do it, have it, be it whatever "it" is. If you can't think of an area, then pretend there is an area in your life where you are just completely sure of your ability and capacity in a positive way. Imagine what is happening to the matrices of your being – your energy field, the spin and velocity, the diameter and color of the electrical and magnetic field of your every cell and of your whole body. States that you move into, states you assume, states you make normal for your being all affect every level of your make-up from the energetic, atomic, psychological, to the cellular and biological. The faculties of your mind and the rhythms of your heart are aligned in unique and recognizable ways when you are in states that are supportive of success. There is always a precise science at work, a precise energetics at work in bringing about the ends you desire in your heart.

For instance, persistence, consistency, and continuity are energetic mechanisms that move you into the field of whatever desired outcome you have chosen. Persistence is a chosen state wherein you continue to orient yourself in the same direction as it relates to your desired outcome. When you are in the state of persistence, come what may, your focus is singular and directional. The experience of persistence, which we traditionally describe as a psychological resource, has itself specific configurations of being. What does it feel like to persist in something? You can feel into that – you can walk right into the field effect of that state and utilize it in your experience. The same is true for making some desired end continuous in your perceptual framework. Continuity is a resource you apply wherein you continue to insert the desire for some outcome in your everyday experience. Instead of desiring it one moment and forgetting about it the next, through the use of continuity, you continue to bring through and anchor the desire for that outcome. This is a creative effort, to continue to desire something, to persist in moving toward it, and to be consistent about wanting to anchor it in your personal reality field, all work together to give your dreams physical form. When you continuously spin your heart and mind in the way of your desired end, your reality field responds by bringing the components and structures of that desired end into view. This physical science of heart and mind is always at work. Expression, whether of success or not, always utilizes principles of physics and math. There is nothing that is happenstance about it.

If you were to right now put all the forces of your heart and mind behind the realization of your success, what do you move into and what moves into you?

You are a field of Consciousness, and the outcome you desire is also a field of Consciousness. When you move toward something, that something also mutually moves toward you. This mutuality of Consciousness is always at play, and you can bring conscious awareness around that movement to notice not only how you are moving toward your desired end, but also to notice how the field of your desired end is in movement toward you as well. What you experience as synchronicity, the cooperation of events, the coincidence of circumstance are all indicative of the mutuality of creative expression – wherein what you express is also expressing you, the field you desire to be in is also desiring you.

If you pay attention to how your own creative being works, you will notice how your heart at the centre of your chest bubbles up with life when you are focused on the possibility of your fulfilment. Your heart revels in the consumption of this energy of "yes it's mine, yes I can have it, yes I can be it, yes I can do it." There is an opening that transpires, and an elevation of your whole circuitry. You come into a new state of harmony, coherence, resonance. You can feel it. Your whole being hums to the rhythm of possibility and the experience of this is often very uplifting. You feel elevated. You feel light. You feel open. You feel expanded. You feel unfolded. It's as though everything about you opens up like a lotus flower. There is a physics to that, an energetic equation at work that is organizing and reorganizing not only your personal field of energy but the whole field of interconnected life in which you are. Feel into the reality "yes it's mine, yes I can do this, yes I can be this, yes I can have this" – that resonance, that space, that change you feel 360 degrees all around you is a change of state, a change of resonance.

What do you feel would happen if you sustained this state, this spin of your heart-mind field?

When you continue to live in this state of harmonizing with the desired end, your mind begins to develop a more precise focus and gains more steadiness. It begins to habituate the state in such a way that it becomes your new baseline, your default. Your go-to thoughts now predominantly become that of the possibility of your desired end. Your awareness is more readily accepting of confirmation, of the waves that echo the reality of your fulfilment. Your concepts change. Your vision evolves, becomes more intricate. Your words change; you speak differently as it relates to your desired outcome. Your tone changes.

Every part of the body begins to learn about the field of your desired end as you tune into it, as you turn your attention toward that field. The body encodes information right along with the heart and mind. The senses, your neurology, the cells and muscles of the body are all as much a part of the change and movement into the desired end as are the heart and mind of your being. Nothing is being missed. Everything about you and around you is a participant in the change. You begin to encode new frequencies. You begin to translate and perceive a different range of frequencies that construct the field of your desired end. The cells of your heart, mind, and body all alter and are altered by the changed states you have made your new home.

All these changes are pointing to a change not only in your neurology but more pointedly in where you are referencing from in Consciousness, as it relates to your desired end. Your location in Consciousness, your IP address as it were, has changed. There is more certainty in your voice, more definition in your new boundaries of being, in this new resonance of self you have brought into being. In this journey, the desired outcome evolves into an expected result. The sustained desire, the accessed state, turns itself into the expected event. The preferred outcome is no longer something you desire to experience but becomes something you expect to experience. This solidification, this crystallization takes place in the inner realms of being. And if you observe the psychological journey of Consciousness you will witness this psychic alchemy taking place.

There is a sort of endurance that's at play in creating a stable focus, a stable state of knowing that fulfilment is your every right. Stability is a useful measure of where you are located in relation to your desired end. Behind the curtains of Consciousness, the manifestation of any desire moves from a fuzzy unstable bubbling up of energy and information to steady streaming of synchronicity and events that form the complete picture. It's like what happens when you change the radio dial to find the right station. There are moments when you just reach static, and as you keep turning the dial, you begin to slowly tune in to the right channel range. You begin to hear the broadcast, and as you keep turning, it becomes clearer and clearer until you have perfect reception.

The contents of the mind reflect this journey. Initially, in the fuzzy states of manifestation, the mind is filled with a mixture of thoughts that either affirm or deny the possibility of the desired end. As you sustain your awareness in the reality of your fulfilment, a certain level of energetic solidity and clarity begins to form. Things begin to come into better focus, and you become better tuned into the frequency range that is broadcasting the desired end you wish for. You ultimately begin to stand and walk across the energetic bridge you have projected in front of you.

At such a point, there is an inherent refusal to put down the idea, to put down the desire. You are really tuned in to the field of your desired outcome. Your attention becomes absorbed in the reality and inevitability of fulfilment that being distracted, scattering your attention into counterproductive thoughts, or giving in to discouragement is no longer optional. Attention stops being frayed, the forces of your heart and mind no longer sputter but are rather collectively directed, all inner technologies flowing, spinning, organizing in support of the ends you desire to experience. Coherence, congruence, alignment, all point to this ability for all of your gears to unify in purpose and in direction.

You can measure where you are in relation to your desired end by noticing where you are on this evolution and revolution of resonance. Look and locate yourself on this move from the fuzzy static states to the clear solid states of being. By looking at the overall feeling that arises as you look at your desired outcome as well as the mental content that begins to come into your awareness, you can track, locate, and recalculate your route on your apparent journey into the field of your desired outcome. Your words, your thoughts, the overall language and tone of where you are now will indicate to you where you are holding yourself in relation to the desired ends. Language is not language, thoughts are not thoughts, everything is sound, a specific geometry of energy and information you are emitting and holding yourself in. Observing the sounds you are making will allow you to recognize and measure where you are in relation to the end you desire. Perform the measurement and you will see and observe where you are on your success route.

No matter what, you must keep walking in the reality field of your desired outcome.

What does that mean? It means don't give up. Persist. Persevere. Keep your attention on the destination, your eyes on the road, and your heart in the space of the desired end being a fixed location. It will unfold, the timing of the unfolding is related to the clarity of your resonant movement in the Field. The more you stay on the journey, the clearer the path becomes, and the more patterns organize and reveal themselves in support of your realization. Stay the course and continue to pay attention to your participatory role.

Feel yourself into this re-tuning: *all that I thought was impossible or out of reach, now comes to pass. I now fully stand in the centre of my fulfilment.*

Let this sound into every cell of your whole being.

It may at first take conscious effort to notice and put to work the energetic mechanisms of success within yourself. You will notice that through practice the same parts that felt like unfamiliar motors within you will feel progressively natural and organic to initiate as you move into new fields of success and fulfilment. Where you have consciously succeeded, you will have created the awareness to employ those mechanisms to varying degrees in new platforms of experience. How you've learned to do one thing becomes how you organize yourself to do everything else. Walking this path of success and fulfilment consciously then becomes a lifelong journey instead of the experience of short-term fulfilment and quick gains. The internal tools and resources you access benefit you and support you in every facet of your experience, even though for right now you are shining the light of your awareness onto them as they relate to the fields of success and fulfilment. There comes a point and there will come a moment where being successful and fulfilled are no longer about specific achievements but about an overall Consciousness and way of being in the world.

Success and fulfilment really don't have a final destination. It's ultimately about the journey of success itself. Success leads to more success and the journey carries on expanding and evolving itself into more complex expressions of Consciousness. While the goals or specific ends change, the mechanism, the path, the journey both within yourself and externally continue on with no end in sight. This is both the commitment and exhilaration of the process. The more you know and recognize the processes of your own being in success Consciousness, the more you will utilize them, and the more you utilize them, the more you will move into bigger and better fields in which to put them to work. It is a creatively thrilling ride every step of the way.

Resonance

To succeed in any way is to exceed and transcend the self you are now and materialize a new self, a new pattern, resonance, and calibration of Consciousness. You then express this new Consciousness as a new experience, a new world. Being a new self isn't hard work. It doesn't take years and years of practice to cement. In entertaining these ideas, you are already forming the foundation for the emergence of this new self. In contemplating these ideas and playing with the possibilities of continuous fulfilment, you are already setting up the internal conditions necessary to allow this new self to emerge.

You are already many selves, the upbeat self, the relaxed self, the easy-going self, the "I have to fix everything" self, there are endless variations of being-ness that you make use of day in and day out. All of these selves were formed as you needed to form them. They came into being as you needed them to come into being. Sometimes it only took one emotionally intense moment to form them. At other times it took a single light decision. Yet at others, circumstances around you influenced you into forming them. Being a new self, one that resonates at the level of continuous success and fulfilment is formed like all the others – through a decision, through an emotionally intense moment, or through deliberate mental and emotional rehearsal where patterns of thinking and feeling are set to run on a loop, on repeat.

The substance of the Universe is Consciousness, and Consciousness organizes itself into different frequency ranges to create the multitude of forms or patterns you see and don't see all around you. Everything in life is about resonance, frequency, and velocity. Everything has spin. Everything has momentum. Everything unfolds itself into and within a specific range of frequencies infinitely birthing patterns within patterns. And so everything is about this oscillation, waving, or undulation of Consciousness. Abundance, happiness, success, or health, are states of Consciousness first before they are manifestations. Before they manifest, these are fields of resonance, patterns of energy or oscillations of energy and information that you come into harmony with. You integrate into the matrices of your being these fields and then express them onto the screen space of your waking world. It is the establishment of these resonances in your being that first births a self that is a match to these qualities of abundance, happiness, success and health. That newly formed self then brings your reality to reflect them. The self you are being is the cause, and your reality is the reflection in the mirror.

It is the same for your desired outcome. Before your desired end is a manifested sequence of moments, it lives contained in and as a field of resonance. It is an un-collapsed event of a particular quality. You can call this a probable event or a potential reality, yet it is very much a real pattern or image in the Field. Whether or not you are listening to a specific radio channel, it is continuously broadcasting its programs. Whether or not you are paying attention to your desired outcome, it continues to exist as a resonating field of light and information in the vast Field of limitless potential patterns.

It's up to you to move yourself into the states of Consciousness that are in harmony with the desired end. You are always resonating with something. You are always resonating as some quality of Consciousness. You are always existing in relation, and so resonance, to something. Even now, you are resonating in a specific way or within a specific range of frequencies when it comes to your physical, psychological, emotional, relational, financial, or social life. Whatever your resonance is, is drawing content or substance from the field of energy and information that it is a match to. Everything is allowed in the Field. The Universe raises itself into events and circumstances, as your mirror to show you every angle of who and what you know yourself to be. You are plugged into and plugging into a specific matrix of being that is feeding and sourcing your reality, through your resonance. The ideas, beliefs, definitions, feelings that are a reality or a source of truth for you aren't really yours. They belong to the field you have plugged into, the field you have harmonized with, in your experience of physical life.

When you live in the feeling of already being, or having, or doing whatever it is you desire, when you live in the feeling of its possibility, you are resonating states that match the desired outcome. You are plugged into the matrix of fulfilment as it were – the living field in which your desired end is already a reality. Think of the creative Field as having an infinite spread of floating program bubbles beyond time and space, that contain their own source codes, contents, patterns. Think of blood cells floating in a sea of plasma. As you collect and integrate templates of being in physical reality, you attune yourself to these bubbles and begin to source ideas, thoughts, beliefs, definitions, identities, images and so on from them. You inform them, you feed into them, and they, in turn, inform you and feed into you. It's that reciprocity of conscious systems at play.

Ultimately what you experience as your world is the resonance of the self you are being. Again this pattern of self doesn't belong to you any more than the air you are inhaling and exhaling. It is a pattern in the field that you for right now are consuming and being consumed by, that you have crystallized or superimposed upon the electrical and magnetic grids of your multi-octave being. What you are is the awareness at back of all patterns, the spacious, atmospheric life force that supports and upholds all patterns. So you feed on patterns of self and temporarily become them. And what you are in Consciousness, you will experience in manifestation. What you are in Consciousness, you experience in outcomes, circumstances, conditions, and relationships. As you change your resonance, by changing this self pattern, you are entrained with, your personal world also changes.

You cannot receive outside of your resonance. You cannot contain what you are not a match to. Even if you momentarily attached to it, it will not stay because you do not have the internal resonant architecture to integrate it. Like the cell membrane that doesn't allow unrecognizable substances to enter into the cell, your personal energy field will not allow entry of realities that you are not in resonance with even if they land right on top of you. Think of your personal energy field as your own cell membrane designed to protect you from "unwanted" energies and to control what can and cannot enter into your personal reality matrix. What you allow to resonate within you is what is projected on your screen-space of experience. Only realties that match the patterns of energy you have encoded your being with, only realities that match the energy codes written on the walls of your internal environment, are allowed to enter into your conscious awareness.

Any doubt, fear, apprehension, frustration, impatience or any other pattern of thought that contradicts your fulfilment is letting you know that you are not in harmony with the field of your desired outcome. Such emotional currents communicate to you that you are not letting that reality in. If you were already anchored and located inside the field of your desired outcome, such patterns of fear, doubt, and apprehension would not arise. It is only when you are locating yourself as separate or external to the desired end that such reflectors of separation or resistance make themselves known to your awareness. To be located inside the reality of your desired outcome means that you as Consciousness have immersed yourself in the reality of the desired end. Regardless of your present environment, in mind and heart, you are already there, you have already arrived into that desired reality. You can feel it, taste it, and sense it with your internal antenna. You know it is there all around you already. It's tangible to you even though your physical eyes don't see it yet. All of the patterns of thinking and feeling that arise are an indicator in this way. These indicators let you know whether or not the new self that you are organizing as is a match to the field of experience in which the desired outcome exists. Every feedback you get in terms of thoughts, emotions and so on is like a Universal Positioning System (UPS! Special Delivery) letting you know where you are located in relation to the field of your desired outcome.

If you were to map out your dominant state of Consciousness what would you say it was? Where do you reside predominantly? Is it something that wavers or are you in some space consistently? It's useful to notice what your starting point is either in general or in relation to something specific you desire to bring to form in your world. Look at the relationship you have to the outcome and anything else similar to it. Notice the resonance you hold and if you recognize that it is not one that serves your goal, change it by beginning to organize and attune yourself to the desired field itself. How do you do that? By first asking questions and locating what the field you'd rather be resonating with and as is all about. You can ask yourself: *where am I right now as it relates to this and where do I want to be?* You read yourself, you energetically locate yourself and then make the adjustments. As you have the capacity to move yourself into any desired state, once you identify where you are and where you desire to be, then it's a matter of moving yourself into the desired state. Nothing can actually stop you from making a state change. If you are curious enough and are willing enough, you will never have to tolerate and keep yourself in states that neither reflect nor support the realization of your success.

It's not the "other" in the relationship you modify but rather the modification of resonance happens in your end of the equation. It's not about what's at the other end of the stick – the other person, situation, circumstance or condition. "They" are not what matter or materialize as the matter of your experience. When you change where you are holding yourself, when you change the pattern of self you are organizing as you change where you are bonding with that "other" from. That change in relationship, that change in the angle of how you are plugging into something, is manifested as a change in the quality of the bond and so ultimately the manifestation of the experience. When you change the resonance of the self you are being, you will draw new patterns that match that new self to you. When you change the self that you are being, those patterns or bonds that are not a match to this new self will either shift their own resonance to match yours or they will fall away.

Now this "other" can be anything – it can be a situation, an event, an object, some scenario, another person or group of person's, an organization, a government – it can be anything. And the relationship you have created internally through the thoughts and beliefs you've been merging with in relation to that "other" is what points to the resonance you have been keeping active inside of your personal field of being. If what you want to observe is something different "over there" then what you want to do is modify or alter the self you are being "over here". Because the way this pattern of self that you currently are is plugging into this something is going to be different from the way a different resonance of self is going to plug into this something. The energy is different. The interpretations, definitions, expectations, beliefs, patterns of thinking and feeling are different. The angles and orientation are different. What changes is the point of reference, and yet that change in point of reference is a change in energy. As everything is multidimensional in nature, nothing actually has to change itself, only the angle with which it is being looked at needs to change for something different, something already contained in the holographic appearance to come to light, to come to manifestation. This may seem a bit unclear, that nothing has to change and yet by looking at it from a different angle it does look and feel completely different. Think of a Rubik's cube, depending on the angle you look at it, you're going to see a different color or a different set of colors. The cube has always had all six colors, but you'll only see one or one combination depending on which side of it you face. This is a simplified analogy to illustrate the point that all that you see and perceive has many sides to it that you don't have access to because of your angle of observation, because of the energy of your current self. Change that angle, change your energy and you'll move yourself into a different location from which to observe your environment. In that change in location or position of observation, everything will look and feel different.

Your resonance then is an indication of multiple factors – your psychological structures in the form of beliefs and your angle of observation, the perspectives you have assumed as you look out onto your environment and world. The higher your perspective, meaning the broader and more inclusive it is, then the more elevated your energy and the higher the frequency range of your resonance. It is always the resonance that you have created that is reflected back to you – for always, your resonance precedes manifestation, the reflection.

The outward focusing of awareness tends to create the impression that things "out there" exist as separate and independent of the you that is doing the observing, witnessing, watching, registering. The continuity of self into world is overlooked and the world is taken to be something that is happening external to the self you are being. This is that self-exclusion pattern rearing its beautiful and comical head. Recognize that the personal boundary you experience, the sense of a personal self, is an experience that can be faded out as you expand your points of reference and as you diminish the activity in certain parts of the brain. The world "out there" and the world "in here" are not as separate and distinct as this self-reference filter makes them seem. Resonance isn't contained to a you inside a body. Resonance localizes itself in an apparent you and extends itself out 360 degrees onto the screen space of your waking world. Everything is an inside job and so it's always under the hood of self you want to take a peek to tinker and toy with how you are doing you.

To get yourself back into resonance, you can **repeatedly** ask yourself the following until you feel yourself back in the desired space again – you can literally track and be aware of a change in resonance:

What does it feel like inside the time and inside the space of my already being/having/doing this desired end?

Step into the space this type of question leads you into. Ask more open-ended questions that guide you right back into the center of your desired reality. What would it look like? What would it feel like? What would you hear? What will you see? What else? See and feel the images and sensations of your desired end and let yourself become immersed in their reality until you are fully merged and fused with the experience. When you achieve this, your environment will fade away, and you'll experience yourself once again internally feeling fully aligned to the preferred outcome. Persist in the resonance of your desired outcome until it becomes your baseline. Some desired outcomes are more effortless for you to move into, and some are not. It's the ones that you really want to experience the most that ask of you persistence, perseverance, and endurance because it is these very desired ends towards which you have created significant resistance. Where you have created separation between "me" and "desired end" is where you will have to wiggle yourself back into coherence, alignment, or harmony. And this is when you can make use of tools like open-ended questions to move yourself into the resonance that magnetizes you into the field of your desired end and makes visible that desired end.

Feel yourself into this re-tune:

I now fully resonate in the space of my desired outcome.

I feel fulfilled.

I feel supported.

I feel universally loved.

Hard-Wired For Success

You will notice that a lot of individuals who have experienced success seem to have a knack for repeating that success. Regardless of what they encounter and irrespective of what comes up for them, they seem to always land back on their feet. One moment you look at them and think, "oh no, they've lost it". And the next they are right back on top as though nothing of the "losing everything" kind ever happened to them. This has nothing to do with chance or coincidence or luck but rather the very hard-wiring of their neurology and the baseline of resonance they have habituated energetically. It is about what they have calibrated their nervous system to notice and the Field that they predominately source out of. When such an individual is met with some new experience, the mechanisms that kick into gear in their being are ones that allow them to assimilate, sift, integrate, and or discard whatever information the new event carries within it. They do this in a way that propels them further into whatever Field they are moving into. The same applies to those individuals you observe coming into great fortune only to be unable to sustain it, maintain it, and regain it once they lose it all. If you look under the hood, they simply did not know how to integrate and be in the space of that new experience. The in-congruence of the self they are used to being with that wealth Field of experience inevitably pops them back out into the familiar, known, and the comfortable world they are used to.

You can be hard-wired for anything. As you move through your experience of waking life, you are recurrently modifying and altering your psychology, biology, physiology, and neurology in response to your inner orientation and your reflected world. You are continuously receiving system updates, rejecting, accepting, and deleting patterns that you find you need or no longer have use for. All of the processes that are going on underneath your conscious awareness are hard-wiring you for a specific range of experiences. You self-correct without knowing that you do. You self-organize and self-adjust without consciously knowing that you do. It is this unconscious structuring of your system that allows you to be in the right place at the right time or in the wrong place at the wrong time and whatever other variations of that are possible.

The formula is always, as within Consciousness so without in the world of form. The world is formed from the within to the without, from the invisible to the manifested. What tells you what you have right now hard-wired yourself for is your current manifested world. Look around, and you will know what fields you have calibrated your nervous system to access, be in resonance with, and source from. What's about you is neither good or bad, it just happens to be one of the many possibilities that you have formed around you and are allowing yourself to be informed by. And in a technologically rich world as this one, with satellite and broadband broadcasts, AM or FM or XM radio, and the internet with its unaccountable sites and databases, it is easy to understand that you can actually allow yourself to be informed by any alternate streaming of information from the creative ocean that forms all worlds. To suggest that there are more channels of information and resonance available to you right now in the Field than the known satellite, broadband TV channels and radio stations combined, is an understatement. To change any manifestation, you have to change the assumed states of Consciousness you hold alive within yourself – and you have more tools than you are aware of to make such state changes reality for yourself.

Who you know yourself to be and what you know yourself to have, these conclusions and understandings are what inform how you organize on all the octaves of your unique expression – from the pattern of self, to the neurology of your physical structure, to the formed events of your world. Changing any part of what you see in your waking life requires a change in the resonance of who and what you know yourself to be. Who do you know yourself to be right now? What are all the definitions you hold about yourself, all the labels, all the measurement sticks for what you can and cannot handle? What do you know yourself to have and not have, both internally and externally? Make note of these points of definition and understand that the solidity of these points, the tangible realness of these points within your Consciousness, is the bases of the world of success and fulfilment you right now know.

It is a change of resonance that transforms the psychology, biology, and neurology of your make-up. Vibration and states of Consciousness that are sustained turn into repeated thoughts, new pathways that form in the brain, new chemical voltage and frequency of your cells, new organizations of your physical structure, new ways of being and behaving in your world. These changes extend out into your extended body of circumstance and condition. As within, so without – for the within is what gives form to the without.

What would it be like if you were to expect success, happiness, and fulfilment at every turn and with every step?

What would it be like if you were a genius at succeeding in your desired ends?

Imagine waking up every day knowing you were going to succeed in your every endeavor, and imagine going to sleep at the end of each day knowing that you were a success in every area of your life. Notice the feeling of that as you step into it with your imagination. Imagine succeeding in the fulfilment of your every dream, whim, and fancy. Imagine everything you could ever dream of always being reachable, always being within your reach. Notice the feeling space this moves you into and recognize that if you are feeling the difference, it is because you are accessing a different range of frequencies, a different field of resonance. And if you would sustain this new range, your world will echo the new states you've accessed.

Magnets don't have to try to draw magnetic materials to them. It is just the nature of their form, to attract, to draw, to bring in. They don't imagine or worry about not being able to do this. It's just what they do. In the same way, what you've hard-wired yourself for, what you've become magnetic to will show up because of your own electrical and magnetic-like being. That you are magnetic, that the very nature of your being has a magnetic quality to it is measurable. What are you magnetic to right now? What do you want to be magnetic to in your world?

Point of resonance: *Things seem to always get better and better for me in every part of my experience.*

Pierce into the energy of this statement and move yourself into it. Wear the energy like a new coat. Look from inside of it. Look out onto your world from within the space of feeling that everything around you is in a constant state of improvement, every part of your life is in a continual state of flowering. Live inside of this feeling, possess it and let it grab hold of you. Notice the way energy moves within you and around you as you are in this space of looking out from this feeling. Feelings are meant to be inhabited when they reflect a new reality, a new way of looking at the world. If this wasn't your predominant place of being, if this feeling isn't a dominant state for you, you'll know it as you reside in it. If this is a feeling that feels natural to you, then it is a feeling or a space of Consciousness you are already drawing from.

When you find affirmative expressions, the point is not to repeat them like a parrot. Repetition can be a useful tool for change, but a more potent form is to move yourself into the energy of the mantra, affirmation, or expressed code. Words are not words, they carry a vibrant living intelligence. They are codes of light and information you use to organize your self and world. One way to entrain to that intelligence inherent to the words that evoke noticeable responses within you is to cycle the words, another way (and there are many ways) is to move yourself into the energy of the words, to sit inside of them. Consciousness can move in to occupy any space. So let yourself live inside the questions, the statements, the codes that are showing up in this space of Consciousness as words and points of resonance. Let yourself experience the affirmations, prayers and mantras. Let them be a felt moment for you. Step into them. Inhabit them. Feel them. Intensify them. Wear them. Let them transform you on an atomic and cellular level. This is what structures new networks in your neurology. The more emotion behind the prayers, mantras and affirmations you cycle or contemplate, the more you really feel the words, the stronger the neurological events that you create in your brain. The stronger the neurological events you create in your brain, the more you've changed and reorganized your brain to a new map of self, relationships, and world. It is the changed brain that ensures a changed reality.

To hard-wire yourself for success then, you must feel successful, you must cycle the patterns of thinking and feeling of being successful. What's the feeling of being successful for you? What's it like to live your desired level of success in all aspects of your life? This feeling you access, step into it again and again until you reach the point where you can't step out of it. Feeling successful, the emotion of it, the mood of it encodes your nervous system for that energy, making you become magnetic to more patterns of light and information vibrating at the level of being successful. To hard-wire yourself for never-ending fulfilment, you must feel fulfilled every which way you look. Changing, updating and upgrading your hard-wiring is not only evolving your perspective, your thinking, your expectations. It is also changing your magnetism, your vibration, your resonance, your very electromagnetic signature in the Field. A changed brain is a changed life.

Changing Your Inner Thermostat

The matrices of your being are naturally inclined to move into more resonant and expansive states of Consciousness. What interferes with this natural gravitational movement toward a sense of total wholeness is the web of beliefs, the grid of constructs that you have formed around the various and many facets of human experience. These definitions, beliefs, assumptions are the very mechanisms that keep you locked into and anchored in the field of your current level of experience. When you loosen those beliefs, those tendencies, the locks that hold you attached to your current fields of experience will fall apart and allow you to organically float toward and into the resonant fields you have identified. If you can look at a field of experience, a pattern of expression, and recognize that it is or isn't for you, you in that recognition have allowed for the space of awareness that can support the materialization of a change in the landscape of your waking experience.

This space of awareness that emerges allows for the expansion of your Consciousness. The expansion of Consciousness happens naturally when you release old programs, in that releasing you liberate energy and elevate yourself into a new level of awareness. The more expanded your Consciousness around some pattern, the faster the spin of your personal matrix, and the faster the spin of your personal matrix, the weaker the magnetic force of your field, making it easier to change, alter, or dissolve the crystallized patterns you experience as beliefs, assumptions, or truths. Once you have created awareness around an assumption, no matter how true, natural, and human it may have once felt to you, you can't ever go back to experiencing it as solid truth. When the false limit is seen as a false limit, when a program is understood to just be a program, it loses all of its suction power, validity, and solidity. More awareness and acceleration of Consciousness that allows for such recognition and movement into new fields, however, is not always a welcome event to parts of your being as it signals a change in the structure and makeup of your being. Your comfort zone is your comfort zone because parts of your nature are accustomed to operating within the bounds of the familiar. The unfamiliar to these parts of self can be seen as a threat to your safety, security and survival.

One of the tools for succeeding in your desired area of success is becoming aware of and then stretching your internal parameters for what can happen in your experience. Stretch your ideas of what can occur not only for you but through you as you make that shift into a new level of awareness and a new playing field. Succeeding means a change in the energy, power, flow, awareness, information, and activity of your being. The flip side to moving into some field of success is that you change. Everything about you, your thoughts, your feelings, your internal narrative, your cells, your level of awareness and presence, your physical structure, the information you are drawn to, your moment to moment activity, your expressions, your expectations, how you relate and who or what you relate to, the amount of energy you run, flow, access – it all changes. Desiring some end and bringing that end into fruition, the journey and process of that always end with a total reconfiguration of your system. Now the question is, are all aspects of your being accepting, willing, and ready for such a complete change? Have you had that preparatory conversation with all aspects of yourself?

Resistance to such a change is often how your conscious mind and physical system retains itself in a state of equilibrium or "normalcy". Have you ever moved through some dramatic change only to feel like it was surreal, weird, confusing, or altogether crazy? Like you sat there wide-eyed and tranced-out wondering what the heck just happened? This is a reflection of the conscious minds resistance to integrating more rapid change because on another level many aspects of your being already knew that change was on the horizon. If things are the same, then things are safe, reliable, predictable, knowable. Ask yourself: what part or parts of me, if any, are wanting to keep things as they are? If you look internally at this with curiosity, you will find the patterns or programs of "why can't I just stay where I am" quietly running somewhere.

This internal reliance or attraction to keeping things the same is configured or imprinted into your physiology to maintain a sense of homoeostasis. Subtle mechanisms of resistance kick into gear when the experience of noticeable change begins to surface. You decide on some experience, you choose to succeed in some way, you rev up your engines for that change in yourself, and you start moving. Then, something inside of you appears to kick-in to get you or push you back into the familiar, the old, the safe, the known. Something internally sounds the alarm and your resolve to move into some new experience dissipates. Anyone who doesn't exercise who has tried to start up an exercise routine likely can relate to this scenario. You start all gung-ho about being more healthy, exercising more, and before that routine is habituated all sorts of things come up, either internally or externally, to stop you from normalizing into a new exercise routine and practice. If you peeked under the hood of your self, you would see the sabotage hamsters running on the wheels of "I don't want things inside of me or outside of me to change".

You can bypass this internal fail-safe program by preparing yourself internally before you begin to take action or as you are taking action into your desired field of experience. One of the many benefits of moving into new experiences through Consciousness first is that you address, modify, and release or deactivate these safety mechanisms before they even move into motion. When you ask yourself "what's it like to already be what I want to be" – the space you access naturally in response to that conscious search begins to internally train you and encode you so that you do not have to push through any programs of resistance. Instead, you are setting and building the necessary structures of self beforehand. You can also take your conscious awareness into the field of your desired success and explore with curiosity as to what this success will translate as and how it will translate to the various portions of your being.

What will this field of success mean to how much energy I access and expend?

What will this field of success mean to how much power I access and flow?

What will this field of success mean to the level of activity in my day to day experience?

What does this field of success require that I become?

What does moving into this field of success mean for my relationships?

How does this field of success relate to my heart?

What's it like to integrate these changes easily?

What's it like to move into these changes with ease, readiness, and effortless adjustment at all the levels of my being?

You can consciously measure and explore what the field of your desired end requires of you by sitting down and really letting yourself sit inside these questions. The more you consciously engage with the field of your desired end, the more you participate in that conversation with conscious awareness, the more fluid your movement into the field of that desired end will be. Success does not come out of the blue. You are always engaged in conversation, you are always in a relationship with spheres and patterns in the ocean of Consciousness. The more you make those conversations and relationships conscious, the easier your navigation becomes as you move from one field into another.

If the Universe is a single harmonious system, a unified expanse of patterns and information, then there is actually nothing to fear, to resist, to beat or bump against – everything is one flow. There is no level of change that means chaos, instability, or disconnection from this unified flow. Change really doesn't have to have a negative spin. All change can be and is useful. All change at every level brings with it new resources, new power, new energy to make use of.

Can you experience rapid change fearlessly without contracting or needing to contract into the familiar?

Can you allow for an acceleration of your fields willingly and in trust of the intelligence that forms you?

Can you experience all change with ease, ready integration, and effortless adjustment psychologically, energetically, emotionally, and physically?

Your experience of growth and integration into new fields, which likely mean new levels of processing, in a fluid and open way relies upon how conscious you make the process and how attentive you are to your own mechanisms of flow and resistance. How you do one thing is actually how you do everything. If you move yourself from one field of experience to another unconsciously, just pushing and forcing yourself into it, what you meet as obstacles "out there" are all the unexamined parts of yourself that are resistant to the change expressing themselves. If a change in experience means "danger" to any part of yourself, that part is going to fight to the death to not have to be moved into danger. Any alignment you see expressed in your world is reflecting the alignment between your heart, mind, and every aspect of your being. And it is the same for any misalignment you experience in your moment to moment reality. You want to take the blindfold off and drive into the fields you desire with all the lights turned on and with all your parts looking in the same direction.

Develop a willingness and readiness to embrace the change in your signature frequency, in your baseline rhythm, pulse, and spin. Embrace the level of presence that an integration into new fields of experience will bring. Readily and willingly let go of the structures and beliefs that aren't resonant aspects of the spaces of experience you desire to be in.

If you were to right now already be in the field of your desired end, what would you no longer have any need for? What assumptions, thoughts, beliefs, reactions, conclusions, tendencies, behaviours would you no longer have any need for?

If you were to right now already be in the field of your desired success and fulfilment, what would no longer be a part of your day to day routine?

And what thought, emotion, assumption, activity would be a part of your day to day routine?

Explore what you have made change mean.

A change in the level of energy you access, a change in the level of activity that is normal to you, a change in the bandwidth of information you access, a change in the frequency ranges your senses register – what have you made change mean? Explore and notice so that you can bypass the self-preservation tendency that kicks-in in response to changing patterns of self and experience. If what you want to bring about is a new experience of success and fulfilment, that organically translates as a change in many facets of your being and world. And the readiness and preparedness to welcome in that change begin with your creating awareness and expectation around that inevitability of multi-layered change for your being.

KIDEST OM

Make It a Game of Trial & Success

Manifesting outcomes consciously, through conscious participation, is an ongoing experiment for many. The rule book for conscious manifesting is fuzzy, with processes, practices, and new templates being formed and reformed in countless ways and utilizing numberless models of reality and self-creation. Depending on what models and systems have informed your waking experience up to this point, you likely have your own preferred methods for creating shifts, changes, and miracles in your personal world. Whatever processes those may be, and whatever you have gleaned thus far in the game of conscious manifestations, make it a game of trial and success for yourself.

Error and failure, like all other representations of Consciousness, are patterns and not truths or essential ingredients to the experience of growth and expansion. There is no such thing as error outside of the sound pattern "error", and there is no such thing as failure, outside of the sound pattern "failure". The measurements and definitions created and contained within these patterns of sound do not necessarily need to be a part of your recipe for the delicious experience of success and fulfilment. What these patterns point to is nothing that is being defined and confined as a something, an event, a real solid reality. You must be discerning in the patterns you integrate into the matrices of your Consciousness. Not everything available is useful or supportive of the kind of journey you prefer to be on. You can employ more valuable and supportive patterns like "re-calibration" and "feedback' or create your own sound patterns that indicate to you and reaffirm to you that this is absolutely your game to play, with your own rules, and in your own way if you so choose. Alternatively, you can tweak the energy behind "error" and "failure" to be energizing by creating new energetic associations, new frames, for those patterns. You have options and the means to re-pattern any pattern or create new patterns altogether. Have you considered the numberless individuals who have moved into new fields of experiences effortlessly, organically? A flower doesn't have to try to bloom through trial and error, or through the process of utilizing mechanisms of failure. Given the right circumstances and conditions, it naturally and organically unfolds itself petal by petal, into the varying levels of expression that you observe as the flower. It does this season after season. The evolution of success, any success, in your experience, can be like the natural unfolding of a perfect and complete pattern. If that's what you choose.

Consider that the seed pattern of any desire already contains within it its perfect unfolding. The very desired outcome you've defined and clarified for yourself already contains within it all the codes needed to automatically and effortlessly write itself into manifestation. From this angle, you're not making anything happen. You're not having to try and put the puzzle pieces together yourself. You're a portal, an entry way to allow this whole and complete pattern to flow through you and all other points of Consciousness involved in the materialization of the pattern. There is no trying and there is no failing. The recipe, instructions and the ingredients are already created and held within the membrane of the desire.

It's very helpful to consider all of the patterns, definitions, constructs on success, and what it means and takes to succeed, you've validated and activated in your field of perception. Looking at the constructs you have made to be real and right for the experiences of success and fulfilment, you can consciously do away with the constructs that look and feel like they are actually energy drains rather than energy gains to your experience. Where they are gains, you can keep them active. Where they are drains, you can tweak them, release them, or create new patterns to replace them altogether.

Take your list of constructs you have formed around success and fulfilment. If you don't have one ready to go from the short game earlier in the book, create one. The more you get to know your existing template, the more awareness you build around it, the more power you give to yourself to change what needs changing and to amplify what needs amplifying. Of all the concepts, rules, "this is what it takes to succeed" assumptions, which are the ones that support and accelerate you into the experiences of success and fulfilment, and which are the ones that slow you down, that slow down the very velocity of your personal energy field? Which ones fuel you and which ones hold you back? Which ones help you play at the level you desire to play and which ones keep you playing smaller than you want? You'll know and recognize them by how you feel when you relate to those constructs. If your constructs connect you to possibility, to flow, to your magnificence and capability, to your vast innate intelligence, then these are keeping you open and expanded. If your constructs keep your Consciousness playing in the fields of self-doubt, incapability, un-resourcefulness, stagnation, weighted-ness and the like, then your constructs are keeping you contracted.

You are at all times in reach of infinite flow, infinite intelligence, and unlimited resources. Twenty-four hours a day and seven days a week you have unlimited access in all directions of experience. Think on what it means to have infinite access, never-ending access. The tap of intelligence and energy is never turned off or diminished in its flow. Knowledge, insight, talent, capacity, resources are not reserved for a select special few. They are equally accessible to all and are codes of potential within every being. The question is, are you connected to this recognition or recognitions like it in your day to day experience? In all directions of life where you cast your attention, is this an awareness you make use of?

A process of examining your constructs like this is similar to cleaning out your refrigerator – as you begin to sort through the boxes and tubs of stuff in your conceptual fridge, you will recognize what's spoiled, what's good, and what's altogether unrecognizable. This is likely going to be different for every individual. A useful construct to one person can be a dis-empowering one to another. It's all relative to the models and systems that currently inform your perceptual matrix and to your current level of psyche development. So taking on this exercise, making it your own, is a very personal process of conceptual spring cleaning. At the end of your cleaning and clearing process, see if what you have set up for yourself is a game of trial and success. And if it isn't, re-define and re-frame the constructs that can turn the game you are currently playing into one that is more uplifting, energizing, and fun.

KIDEST OM

Success Builds On Itself

The field of any pattern in a conscious and living system builds on itself, grows on itself. Everything conscious expands and enhances its nature through perpetuation and reinforcement. This is true also for the resonant patterns of fulfilment and success. The more you notice how successful and fulfilled you already are for instance, the more you reside in that awareness or space of Consciousness, the more you experience more success and more fulfilment.

How are you already successful?

How have you already experienced fulfilment?

What were those moments, events, images, feelings like?

Focus on this and give it your full attention again and again. Remind yourself of the energy and content of those moments you've already lived and have allowed through your being. Energy flows where attention goes, and whatever has your attention also begins to feed you more information to enhance your view. The more you give your attention to a field or pattern, the more that pattern goes into high definition mode. You see and experience its reality with sharp awareness – it's as though the pattern begins to move through resolution upgrades and you become aware of the more intricate patterns and colors that make up that field, event, or pattern itself. Energy follows attention, which then accesses or adds more information to maintain that attention. It's an unfailing feedback loop. In the same way, you build muscles or new neural pathways, you tend to internally build circuits of success that grow and create more bundles of success circuits. Success naturally and organically builds on itself and enhances itself.

The more you are attentive to the energy of success, the feeling of it, and the materialization of it in your experience, the more you experience more moments of that same field and feeling. When you pay attention to your success, other moments of success, you may have forgotten about suddenly pop themselves back into your awareness. Like the patterns the ripples on the surface of water form, it's as if fields expand themselves in outgoing concentric circles. When you resonate within the field of already being successful and already being fulfilled, this state or feeling moves out of you in ripples that grow in their circumference as they move away from you. And in that expansion, more comes into view for you to be aware of.

Your experiences mimic that same pattern wherein one success, and your awareness of it, leads to a greater success, which leads to even greater success and on and on it can go. Resonant outcomes multiply themselves as you remain in a coherent state of being, one in which you are aware of the power of your own heart and mind, and one in which you are ever attentive to the field of success and fulfilment that has already made itself available to you. One way to grow your experience of success and fulfilment is really just this exercise of awareness and resonance. In your focus and celebration of where you have already succeeded, you open up to allow more reflections that reaffirm and perpetuate the reality of the success Consciousness already within you. Nothing is in the way of that success and fulfilment especially if you are orienting yourself to tune into it.

The awareness of noticing where you are already successful also deepens the possibility of your success. Not only does success build on itself externally, but it primarily does so internally. It is the deepening in the spaces of Consciousness you reach as it relates to how successful you can be, how fulfilled you can be, that bring you into a state of knowing that your fulfilment is inevitable. Success deepens itself and builds upon itself from within you, from inside of you and out onto the screen space of your waking life. Once again, there is nothing in the way of your internal explorations of that experience. Nothing can stop you from noticing the spaces in which you are already successful and have already succeeded. What happens when you pay attention to these fields? What feelings take over and fill your field of perception? The more you go inward to feel into states of success, the more you go inward to feel into the structuring of success and fulfilment, the more you will notice a clearing of paths and pathways in your waking life. The Field does not differentiate between past success, present success, and future success. The language the Field understands is resonance, and resonance is created in all direction without forward, backward, or sideways movements being relevant. It doesn't matter where you focus, as long as the focus you are extending is bringing you into the oscillations of Consciousness the Field around you understands, hears, and receives, as success resonance. And where you have accessed and sustained that resonance, you have brought to life fertile ground in which new patterns of success will stand to dance upon.

It is the deeper reach inside yourself, in the interiors of your awareness and field of Consciousness that allows you to move into states of knowing, states of an embodiment of the patterns that support and catapult you into experiences of success. As the states of already being successful and already being fulfilled crystallize in your awareness, as they become states that feel as solid as the ground you walk on, you move out of thinking and believing, and into feeling and knowing the solid reality of them. Living them in your three-dimensional world follows shortly, if not immediately.

The more you know that you can have whatever it is that you desire, the more you become saturated by the field of its possibility. You exude possibility. You exude probability. You radiate the definiteness of fulfilment at every turn. This is a space beyond mental determination. It is a space of aligned fields of being that fluidly move you into the right spaces, circumstances, situations so that the reality and realization of your fulfilment are continuously in your awareness. It's as if the whole entire field of creative intelligence is whispering to you that, yes, in fact, you can do whatever it is that you desire to do, you can have whatever you desire to have, and you can most definitely be whatever you desire to be.

Everything builds on itself in this way – the fields and patterns, the states of Consciousness amplify and solidify themselves through the power of awareness and attention. Success feeds on success. Fulfilment feeds on fulfilment. And all adds to itself through this reciprocal feedback of attention consuming energy to expand its field of inclusivity on what is possible, what is probable, what is inevitable.

No one actually succeeds alone in this interconnected creative web of Consciousness. Whatever success and growth you see "over there" or "out there" is not the success of a separate independent so and so. You are not a separate and independent "me" over here witnessing the success of a separate independent "them" "over there". Collapsing the illusion of separation in the observation of the success and levels of success that surround you will allow you to access and make use of the layers upon layers of patterns available to support you in your unique expression of success and fulfilment.

You are not separate and independent of anyone's success – past, present, or future. In the unification of your perception, you know that everything is in constant demonstration of the continuity of your own being. You are everything that you see. You are raised as "they over there" are raised. You are elevated and expanded as "they over there" are elevated and expanded, for in this field there is actually no fixed boundary that separates, no end to the you that you take yourself to be and no beginning to the "they" that they appear to be to you. All is one undifferentiated Field. And bringing this recognition to light in yourself will give you access to resources that you otherwise keep yourself unaware of.

Take the individual or individuals that are a representation of great success to your point of reference. Bring them to mind and let them stand in front of you in all their successful glory with all the representations of the success they have achieved behind them. Now, remove the lines between "me over here" and "them over there" that you have drawn and are maintaining in your own perceptual framework. See the continuity, the unified flow that is present between you and "him", "her" or "them". Now stay with that fluid and continuous sense of being. Whatever level of success anyone has achieved in your world reference, is your own, is an extension of your own being, so yes, you can naturally and organically express and bring to fruition something similar or of your own.

Now imagine the success of the Universe as it has unfolded itself into the seen and unseen worlds around you. As you hold the vast cosmic sea of intelligence in your mind's eye, remove the boundaries you have formed around "me over here" and "the Universe all around me". Ancient and wise, vast and resourceful, powerful and without limit, intelligent and aware, you are forever at one with every Field of success you can imagine and that right now rests beyond the reach of your imagination.

KIDEST OM

The Power of Attention

Attention is a quality of awareness. When awareness is focused on a specific direction or in a particular way, we call that attention. If someone says to you: "I need you to give me your full undivided attention right now," you suddenly do something to adjust your focus, your attention as you respond to their request for your whole field of focus to be collected around them and whatever they are saying to you or about to tell you. No one really taught you to do this. No one really told you or taught you what it means to put your attention on something. It's always been something you do – it is something all conscious living systems do naturally to adjust to their environment and the world around them.

Deep listening is also called attentive listening. And this is an important marker. There is a depth of focus in attention, a deeper engagement with what's being paid attention to, one that is different from the superficial wandering or scanning aspect of conscious awareness. Attention, when turned on fully, requires a certain degree of your being, being fully present, your collecting all of yourself into the moment. The mind is made to cease in its wanderings, thought activity lessens if not altogether dissipates and even your breathing is modified.

This kind of attentiveness is, in a way, like a focused ray of the sun. It is active living energy being beamed in a specific direction, and it is this directing of aware energy that brings something into your full awareness. Attention reveals what is hidden, forgotten, overlooked, or even ignored. It casts light wherever it is directed to make information available that otherwise would not have been, whether locally or non-locally, whether in your immediate reality or in others. What has your attention energetically? Take a moment to notice. Now, what has your attention mentally? And what has your attention emotionally, or physically, socially, or financially, relationally? You'll know something has your attention when you notice thought content, sensations or emotions arise as you shift focus from one area of experience to another. Look at where these questions take you and take notice of what you notice. Look at how your attention moves as you are directed to the various spheres of your waking experience. Your attention moves like a beam of light to bring into view whatever Field or experiential terrain you are directing it toward. Energy follows your attention. Light follows your attention. Revelation follows your attention. Where you put your attention is where things begin to come under the light of it. Every path is brought to light by the power of your sustained attention.

When something occupies your attention, you begin to become absorbed in it just as it becomes absorbed in you. Attention is like a doorway – it is how you enter "other" fields, and it is how things begin to enter the field of your awareness. You are suddenly more aware of the things your attention is on. If you move your attention to your feet, you are suddenly more aware of the sensations in your feet. If you move your attention to the table, you are suddenly more aware of what it looks like, how big it is, and so on. If you move your attention down to your spiritual heart at the centre of your chest, your awareness and field of perception changes and you become aware of your world from this location. It's useful to notice how you do you, how the various mechanisms of your being work, for in that learning you gain more knowledge of how your world comes to look and feel the way it looks and feels.

Resonance is also a function of sustained attention. What doesn't have your attention will not entrain with you. What doesn't have your attention will not enter your field of experience to harmonize with you. What doesn't have your attention or what never had your attention will not integrate itself into the matrices of your being. Attention is the hook and line of bringing something into your experience, for the moment something gets your attention that something is also being attentive to you. Harmonization, coherence, resonance all have a component of attentiveness at work in them. Put another way, attention is how Consciousness recognizes itself through the appearance of multiplicity and begins to unfold and reveal itself to itself.

The revelatory nature of attention is clear, the more you remain aware of or attentive to some desired outcome. With your sustained attention, things begin to snap into place and click into position. Where, at first, there appears to be no way and no how, with sustained attention, the means and the way begin to take shape before your eyes. Through synchronicity and coincidence, you start to notice and participate in a network of circumstances that begin to make clear the way to your fulfilment. This is all the outcome of your sustained attention, your continuing to give the reality you desire validity and solidity by giving it your attention. It's real. It's solid. It's happening. It has your attention.

The light of your attention reveals what has always been there for you – like a flashlight, you shine the light of your awareness as attention onto the dark field of Unknown patterns. The more you remain in the awareness of your fulfilment, the more that becomes visible to support your fulfilment. There is a reciprocity, a feedback loop at work in the power of attention. When you pay attention to something, you consume its energy, it feeds you. As you are fed by it, it reinforces its reality, validity, solidity. And it carries on until that sustained awareness of a possibility has translated itself into solid reality.

Attention is powerful. Attentiveness is powerful.

A focus of curiosity is helpful. If your attention wanders, then so does your energy. If your attention is scattered, then so is your energy. If your attention is singular like a laser, then so is your energy. How and where you cast your attention determines what you are shining the creative light of the Universe upon, it determines what you're magnetic to, it determines what you are providing fuel for, it determines what you are harmonizing and resonating with, it determines what patterns from the Field you are collapsing or actualizing into your reality.

Feel yourself into this re-tune: *I am attentive to the reality of my fulfilment. I nourish and am nourished by the field of my success.*

There is a great power that awakens in you as you move into the realization that you can have your desired outcome. This begins with a movement of your attention. When you move from wanting your outcome to a deep feeling that you can have the outcome, something shifts in your awareness, in your being. Something wakes up. Energy moves differently, your awareness opens up, and your sense of presence changes.

Take something you want to experience right now and let yourself move into the recognition that you can experience this desired outcome, move into a deep feeling of this sense of "I can". I can have this. I can do this. I can be this. Give your attention to the realization, the feeling, the consideration that you can have this, or do this, or be this.

Notice where that takes your awareness, your focus, your attention. Dwell in that space. If you find it fades, then move yourself into it again.

What can you be?

What can you do?

What can you have?

How much attention have you given these points of focus? Consciously examining and stepping into the deep feeling that you can do, or have, or be something you desire instantly opens you up into possibility states. It doesn't take much to move into a possibility state. All it takes is this shift in attention. All it takes is your own attention shifting to the possibility of your desired outcome.

What's it like inside the space that you can _____?

How does it feel inside the space that you can _____?

This is a different space of awareness than your habituated sense of moving through your world. The things you already know you can do, you are already awake to and so don't give them very much thought or even attention. You just do them. It is in the things you don't yet know you can do or be or have that you want to awaken to. And to awaken to these possibilities takes a shift in your awareness, a move in the orientation of your Consciousness to these untouched territories of being.

You are already in these possibility fields, only you aren't awake in them yet. They are dormant or latent spaces that you haven't blasted the light of your awareness through. So as you make explorations in this way, you begin to shake and wake yourself up in these spaces so that you can start to include them in your field of "things that can happen in my world" so that they too become things you automatically just do. If you've never thought about how you can do something before, that indicates to you that you have not awakened yourself inside that field. You've never entertained it, and so you haven't entrained with it before. When you begin to consider it, when you start to think you can do it, when you begin to look at it with interest and curiosity, it begins to engage with you in the same way. What you flirt with, in Consciousness, flirts right back with you. What you put your attention on, will put its attention on you.

KIDEST OM

Mind Your Physical Mind

Within the greater non-local mind of your being is the physical mind, an organization of Consciousness that allows you to filter through a sea of information to experience the reality, self, and world that you experience. While the greater mind is the matrix of all matter, you can say that the physical mind supports in the ingestion, perception, and projection both of and onto the Field of your experience. It is a very useful and playful living aspect of physical life.

Managing the physical mind is a crucial aspect of success Consciousness. It is a system of circuits that requires monitoring, clearing and updating regularly. You also have to regulate it between activity and inactivity for optimal performance. To do that means you have to begin paying attention to the inner functioning of your physical mind. You want to stay on top of your ongoing internal dialogue, which is an indicator of how much activity you have going on. If your mind is full of chatter, it indicates that the level of activity needs to be regulated. Unchecked this internal chatter can get out of hand and turn itself into an avalanche of resistance that can make your waking experience really uncomfortable. The moment you completely externalize your focus, your mind begins to run reactive to whatever is arising. It's a natural process of conscious focus wherein as you register information, scan your reality field, and move through your moments, reactions, responses, and narratives are generated.

Call this the mind, whatever else you like, or call it ego, but never call it "mine" with any level of seriousness. To take possession of the reactive nature of conscious processing and give it a separate and independent identity is to create fragmentation in Consciousness where there is actually none. Simply recognize and re-organize whatever impressions are formed and forming to suit and serve your desired outcome. Without attachment and personalization, you can move through and navigate this surface activity of Consciousness. If a computer were to take all the registry errors and junk data forming on the hard-drive in the background personally, and take it to mean that all of that meant something about its nature, capacity, and identity, it would experience more system crashes than necessary. That is to say, you are not and never have been this surface activity of waking experience. Mind the physical mind, recognize it for what it is, and interact with it and through it without throwing your whole reference of self into it. You'll likely experience much less resistance, or system crashes, that way.

It is instrumental to maintain a stream of inner awareness of the information your mind is forming in the background. It's always just information before it becomes your perspective or outlook. The way to clear your mental space is to have a portion of your attention focused there, tuned in to the narratives that form and accumulate. You have to recognize the narratives as narratives to be able to relax out of them, witness them and ultimately keep or release them. Stories that don't get any buy-in from you, narratives that you see as just chatter usually dissolve in your awareness before they gain traction and become your outlook or observation. There's always a sliver of an instant in which your awareness is entirely detached from narrative. The gap between thought and awareness is always there for you to leverage so you can consciously fuel and empower only the perspectives arising in awareness that serve you.

Consciousness can generate multiple points of awareness like it's looking at multiple screens or windows simultaneously. You can, in fact, both be aware of "in here" and "out there" at the same time.

Everything is revealed to you when you are attentive to your mind. This alert attentiveness is necessary to navigate yourself into the fields of experience you desire. The way to keep your eye on the road of success is to keep an eye on your mind.

You always have and will always have the power to choose the quality of thoughts, to choose what you set into motion inside yourself. You may not have a choice in the first reactive thought if it's a well-rehearsed response, but you can certainly interrupt the train it can get on and amplify. It takes a certain kind of determination to lead your mind rather than have it lead you initially, usually astray if you're in the habit of not checking in with the internal dialogue now and again. It can be done in any area of your life. You can be the lead, the director, the keeper of your mental landscape. It's not about controlling your thoughts or forcing your mind, but rather through the power of your attention gently directing its focus back into gear toward the reality field you have decided you want to be in. Once you do this gentle nudging, you begin to create new grooves for your mind to extend out through, grooves or pathways of thought that are more conducive to supporting the outcomes you prefer.

NOTHING IN THE WAY

What are the nature of your thoughts right now as it relates to your desired outcome?

What are your impressions, reactions, common internal narratives?

These thoughts being generated are not truths or facts, but the impressions you have adopted or created that have been undirected. You can look at them without judgment or resistance, and begin to direct your mind to flow into channels of thought that are more reflective of the desired outcome. You can ask yourself, "what kinds of thoughts would I rather have popping up and recurring? What kinds of thoughts are more reflective of the experiences of success and fulfilment I prefer?" This psychological rerouting and rewiring is what translates itself as new neural networks in the brain, new channels of flow. And such rerouting of energy begins by your creating space and awareness around the inner narrative that commonly and continuously forms itself as you move through your waking world.

You can move yourself into any situation you desire through this simple practice of keeping an eye on your mind. This is when you enter into the realm of Mastery as you are relentlessly alert to the way energy is moving around you and within you, as well as the way energy is being allowed to move through you. Your mind is influenced by the flow of energy and information in the world. Living in reaction to this flow, you become driven by the outward directed mind. When you live in the state of awareness of directing your mind, however, you gain leverage and influence on how to direct the energy all around you, and how to create new paths of expression both within and outside of you. You are no longer at the mercy of external situations and temporary appearances. Self-mastery on any endeavor begins with this awareness of your mental terrain and what is being allowed to run rampant within it.

It is this minding, this attentiveness that allows you to become single-minded, steady in your focus, stable in your out-looking. It's through this attentive and deliberate guidance of thoughts that you craft your world consciously, intentionally, deliberately. To live on purpose, to live out your intentions, requires this inner authoring, this minding of the mind. It takes practice, commitment, and vigilance if it's not something you already do. It takes a willingness on your part to measure where you are in relation to where you want to be and to listen in on the conversation being stored within you internally about your destination. This internal conversation is creative sound. Everything is creative sound. It's not to be ignored or stamped as "just thoughts" as all sound in the Universe is creative in nature. Thoughts are silent sounds, silent codes of light that still extend out from you and into the Field. Kept memories, kept reactions, kept internal streams of thought are stored information that influences the way you navigate through your waking life and the way you are steered by the fields into which you have placed yourself.

And it is such a level of awareness that makes you indifferent to appearances. You are aware of what you are putting out into the space around you, and you are aware that there are eternal creative principles at work that will bring about the reality of what you are internally in resonance with. As you mind your mind, you will realize there is an inner attentiveness that is always alert to the thoughts that flow in, the thoughts that are kept, and the thoughts that are released. This same attentiveness has full access to the catalogue of memories you're keeping stored in your subconscious and unconscious centers. With a little practice of turning your attention inward, turning the light on inside your mind, you will begin to notice what's going on in there without any conscious prompts. You expand to see more of your inner Witness and work with this inner attentiveness to direct your mind in creative, constructive, and useful ways.

Most people don't consciously choose to be negative, to be home to dense or slow spinning patterns of energies. They are unaware of this inner attentiveness and the freedom to choose what thoughts they can attach themselves to and make their mindset. Every mindset is formed and reformed by the thoughts we consciously or unconsciously put into ourselves. This inner attentiveness isn't a way of being you were taught in school or in childhood. It is a seeing you grow into as you investigate the nature of your being, the nature of your mind. It's an inner alertness that's always been there, but because you haven't looked at it, you haven't integrated its presence into your field of focus.

It is from this inner attentiveness that you have the leverage to release or neutralize any tension whether it arises in the form of fear, frustration, or any other pattern of thinking that negates the reality of your success. It is from this inner attentiveness that you have the means to unlock the memories and filters that no longer serve you. Perspectives, attitudes, experiences don't just emerge out of nowhere, they are first formed in the inner layers of your being, they are first subtle forms of thought that accumulate and crystallize into elaborate stories, grids of light and information, projected on the screen space of your reality.

As you self-navigate through and into your desired fields of success be mindful of the trap of restlessness and distraction – these are both indicators of the undirected mind. Restlessness and distraction diffuse the flow of your focus and attention. Dis-tractability is not a useful resource. Restlessness is not a supportive state. When you find yourself distracted from your path, when you find yourself seemingly thwarted by some apparent obstacle or the perception that things aren't going the way you thought they would, you are in these instants employing resistant mechanisms that keep you from noticing and seeing the clarity of the path before you. The path to success and fulfilment is always clear. The way is already made. The means already provided. Whether or not this is clear to you is a matter of where you have put your own attention and how you are employing the gears of your heart, mind, and nervous system.

You will always notice what you've set yourself up to notice. You will always encounter what you've set yourself up to encounter. Own your mind. Own your focus. Own your attention. Fully occupy these organic technologies of your creative being. Be not distracted from the Fields of your desired experience. Let go of restlessness or any other state that creates discord, when or if it arises and re-engage yourself to the reality of your desired outcome. There is steady diligence that emerges when you let yourself commit and recommit to your desired outcomes as you navigate through the apparent hills and lulls of waking experience.

And yet it will always remain, that all apparent hills and lulls are not at all what they appear to be. See through the mirage of the terrains of waking reality, see through the camouflage, and it will be clear to you that there is nothing, absolutely nothing, in the way. For in this awakened seeing you will realize that the way and whatever appears to be in the way, is you – you yourself are the way.

You yourself are the way.

Follow Your Heart

One of the most useful things you can do is follow the dance of your own heart. There is no other lead to follow, no other thing to take direction from. What speaks in your heart, what calls to you, what pulls to you, this is what you want to pay attention to, and this is what you want to answer to. It's not about the world that appears. It's not about what the world "out there" needs. It's not about the endless concepts and plans your mind can come up with to explain, justify, sort out any part of your experience. It's about what's birthed and being birthed in your own heart. It's born in you for a reason, for reasons beyond the field of your conscious mind and your every day knowing can grasp or reveal. You must move into trusting that voice, surrendering to that voice, letting those inner directives that come through as feeling be the truths on which you take your steps.

You'll always know when it's a heart-nudge, a pull from the field of your heart. You'll always know when it's heart activity whispering in your awareness. It is a noticeably different feeling than mental activity and the suggestions of the mind. Saying yes to what's in your heart, saying yes to not only the possibility but the reality of what's in your heart is probably the most powerful exercise or practice you can take on. Committing to bringing what's in your heart to pass, committing to and persevering in the act of breathing life into the desires that stir within you from deep within the heart is the most important thing you can take on. Authentic self-expression and true self-extension are about the unfoldment of the seeds you have in your heart, the seeds of patterns, the codes of light, you experience as deep desires that flow through you and breathe life into you.

The realization of your heart's desires isn't left up to some outer circumstance or condition. The realization of your heart's desires isn't a gift from some external removed power. It isn't up to things "out there" to bring them to fruition or realization. It isn't up to the Universe to hand them over to you or force them into your experience. You are seeded with these inklings for a reason. It is a gift and responsibility you have given to yourself from the greater realms of existence. It is something you have brought with you into this world experience. Nature, creation, the Infinite Intelligence of this reality field doesn't seem to do anything by accident. There is a precision, a mathematical exactness to the way the world, galaxies, Universes and bodies are organized and expressed. And this same Intelligent organization is what has created the unique pattern of Consciousness that you are, unique with your experiences, assumptions, and more pointedly your innate burning desire and inclination toward some expression.

NOTHING IN THE WAY

Have you ever thought about why it is in your heart to bring about some desired end?

Have you thought about where the impulse originated?

Have you felt into it?

Have you asked what it is that is desiring to unfold through you, from you and as you through these emerging heart-inklings?

You will be able to easily distinguish what's coming out of your mind from what's coming out of your heart. The mind and the heart are different translation centres of awareness, different ports and posts of communication with the Field at large as it were. Most often, what occurs to you from the Heart is something you didn't think of, expect, or anticipate. Usually, when you experience a heart-prompt, it's a movement you didn't construct through logic and reason. And this heart-prompt frequently ends up being a desire, a want, a need, an experience that undoubtedly moves you into a new field of being, a new expression and experience of yourself. The growth impulse is one that comes up and through from the heart.

The self-expression that originates in the heart is one in which when you do step into it fills you with a new sense of aliveness, a new sense of purpose, function, and being all together. It unleashes a new flow of energy in your being, and often when you listen to it, your mind is flooded with ideas, images and insights leading you into your new terrain of experience. Following the heart calls you to listen in regularly to the impulses, pulls, and calls that bubble up within you. The heart isn't an abstract reference for something you can't connect to or access. It isn't allegorical. Within you right here and now, you can move your awareness out of the head or throat or wherever thoughts may be bubbling up from, and down into the center of your chest. As you make this journey of awareness, you will access a space of quietude wherein you can listen to the true desires of your being, the subtle or not so subtle prompts of a broader Intelligence. Your purpose at any stage of your life and development is fully accessible in this central center of awareness. Make this trip often and commune with this center, and you will access fields and grounds that cannot be contained within the confines and spheres of your conscious mind. The heart is a most powerful force in the whole human system, both physically and non-physically. What it reflects and what it allows you to access are realms for which there are currently no concepts.

In many cases, clear distinctions between emotions and feeling aren't offered – the two terms are used interchangeably. There is, however, a distinction between the experiences and qualities of being these two constructs point to. You don't emote into things, but you can undoubtedly feel into them.

While emotions serve as indicators of energy flow through the nervous system and as available energy potential for the nervous system, feelings are powerful conduits of accessing and creating resonance with more of the unseen portions of your reality field. Feelings in one part are a way of sensing into nonlocal terrains like temporal spaces or alternate possibilities. You can feel into your intentions. You can feel into a table, a room, an imagined outcome. You can feel into the energy flow of an environment, whether it's the internal environment of your body or your local community. Through feeling, you extend awareness out like you would your hand when you reach for an object. In a way, your feelings, this ability to feel beyond yourself is like using your psychological, energetic or psychic hands to reach into spatial and non-spatial events.

Feelings, this ability to feel into spaces and fields, are a technology of the heart, and it is a technology that can organize your emotions or bring you into a state of coherence. Just as the mind-awareness extends itself through focus and attention, the heart-awareness extends itself through this technology that is experienced as a feeling. You can feel ahead into the day, you can feel ahead into a situation, you can feel into the space of happiness or joy, you can feel into any direction of awareness and access something, access information, plug into something, some field or current of intelligence and information.

Awareness is projected in any direction to access patterns that are not localized or expressed in your current space-time coordinate through this technology of the heart.

Feelings act as a powerful bridge for awareness, they extend themselves so that you can have something to move through to access information that is "over there" or perceived and experienced as "not here". They are like connector cables – palpable chords you extend and make use of to access and download information from innumerable Fields. The mechanisms and forces of the heart have not yet been studied to the degree the forces, and the faculties of the mind have. And yet, if you take that journey from a predominately mind-based awareness to a heart-centered consciousness, the heart itself will reveal to you the finer or subtler processes it is continuously engaging to power the organization of your reality field and nervous system.

Feelings also indicate resonance, the overall oscillation of your energy field can be felt. If you expand your awareness out 360 degrees around you from the heart, you can feel the movement of the energy field around you and register an overall quality of feeling to the space you inhabit and to patterns you have swirling around in your field. You can even access information about patterns that have not yet come into visibility and are about to and navigate through them. Have you considered what technology is at work to be able to allow you to feel into spaces and fields like this? This is the technology of the heart, and this is only the beginning of what you can come to be aware of when it comes to this center of awareness. It is a powerful technology you can consciously make use of in your success journey.

There is a difference between thinking about something, thinking into something, and feeling about something and feeling into something. These extensions of awareness from different centers of focus are noticeably distinct in what forces and processes they utilize to bring information through into your conscious awareness. They are all useful forces, processes, and technologies, and yet recognizing which processes will yield the most support to your desired experiences is essential. It's like knowing when to use the brake on your car and when to step on the gas – different technologies, all useful, for different functions or toward different ends of what you want to accomplish.

What happens when you feel into the reality field of your success?

What do you access?

Poke around in the field and see what you get. Notice what extends from you and where from you it extends when you feel into a space or field. If you predominantly sense the world through sight or sound, see if you pick up something different as you do this. The more you allow yourself to be aware of this center of awareness at and around the heart, the more you will train yourself to access information, fields, and spaces that are beyond the reach of your conscious mind.

The heart offers itself as an invaluable portal of accessing, tuning into, and attuning into the fields and spaces that best support the realization of your desired end. Listen to it often, daily, make it a practice to quiet down and locate yourself there to then navigate through and into where and into what it directs you. What you access through the heart and what you receive through the heart will never fail in bringing you exactly what you need to make your dreams a reality.

What does it feel like inside the space and inside the time of your already having the desired success?

Peek on in, and feast on the information offered you as you make use of extending the chords of feeling into the fields of your desired success. Such an interaction is what allows you to materialize a journey that is free of incongruous events. The more you plug into and source from the field of your desired success through the power and chord of feeling, through the access centers offered by the heart, the more you allow your reality to reconstruct itself with the energy of that desired field. What you source from is what you are sourced by. And it is the power and technology of the heart that can allow you to transcend the boundaries of your current reality field and tap right into, plug directly into, the body of your desired field of success, right from where you right now appear to be. Beyond time and space, beyond your current coordinate in space and time, the heart gives you access to more points of resonance in support of your desired end than you can imagine.

Drop into the heart.

Expand.

Listen.

Engage.

Resonate.

Manifest.

KIDEST OM

The Power of Preparation

Whatever state of being, whatever resonance you move yourself into, will bring about a matching manifestation. This is the principle that has always governed your reality matrix. Manifestations can only prove the states of being you have made your residence; the fields of Consciousness you have made your home. Nothing is unattainable or out of reach. If you can move into resonance with it, it will materialize itself in your personal experience. And if it has not materialized in your experience, it is because you are not in resonance with it. The creative Field of the Universe is an impersonal one, where all have equal access and availability to any desired end. It is by the resonance you hold that you are fulfilled and it is by the resonance you hold that you are unfulfilled. That is all that is at work.

Any situation can be brought about; any desired end can be materialized or brought into visibility. Nothing stands between you and the desires of your heart. Because you have the power to move into any state of being, any space of Consciousness, you can move into any experience. You have all the power you'll ever need to source and resource the energy, patterns and information necessary to architect your preferred anything. The science is the same, and the continuity of the self you are being into the world you are living is the same. Nothing is actually in the way, for the way, the you that's on the way, and what's at the apparent end are one continuous field of resonance arranging itself into different patterns. The start, the middle, and the end of your journey of success are different arrangements of a range of frequencies that are being formed into the events, relationships, and landscape of your experience.

All insecurity is the distortion of your ever-present success and fulfilment. When you are operating from beliefs, filters, memories or emotion that negate the reality of your wholeness, connectedness, resourcefulness and the like, the flow of energy, intelligence and information is distorted to match your existing blueprints of self, relationships and world. Meaning, you always see the world as you are and not as it truly is. Where wholeness pervades, you see lack. Where completeness is present, you see uncertainty. You see only within the limits of your own emotionalized constructs, constructs you have stamped the stamp of truth upon. The only thing there is for you to do is to see with great clarity how the resonant desired end you wish to have is already given to you, made available, and accessible to you. It can't be any other way.

If you were to right now have the manifestation of your desired end, what would you be feeling?

NOTHING IN THE WAY

This is the feeling you want to live in, this is the field of resonance you want to inhabit. This is the space of feeling you want to source out of and be sourced by. This is the space of resonance you want to be informed by. This is the field of information you want to use to define yourself, your relationships and your world. You must let go of being fully informed by how things appear. You want to construct yourself, your world from and by the energy of your envisioned end.

Can you have perfect trust in what you see and feel from the resonant space of your fulfilment?

Can you allow this energy you access to be as real to you as the world you see formed around you?

One way to anchor this resonance, to encode for this field, is to prepare for your success. What needs to be in place for your reception of the desired end? If the success you desire were to come to knock on your door right now, what would you want to be in place? Put those things in place. Act in preparation of receiving the success you desire. Set up your physical landscape the way you would if you were expecting to have a guest for dinner. When you know something, or someone is coming, when you have an appointment set, you move with the certainty of that happening and act accordingly.

You get ready, you prepare and you behave in line with the certainty of its arrival. The same principle can be applied to the success you desire. The demonstration of preparation communicates that you know you have a set appointment, a set fulfilment. It solidifies the reality of your desired outcome. It crystallizes the resonance of that field into your personal field. It locks and anchors the patterns of that desired success into your perceptual matrix. This activity of preparation is also a great resource for the conscious mind which likes "real solid hard facts" as it gives it "real facts" to reference in the expectation of fulfilment – it completes the circuit of reception when you begin to move and take action in your world inspired by the space of your fulfilment.

Ask: *what do I need to do right now to prepare for this? What do I need to do right now to be ready for this?*

This questing will allow your conscious mind to begin to accept information that is in tune with the field of your success. In the same way you would prepare for a guest coming to dinner, in the same way you would stage your home, clean up, make dinner, and set the table, for that sure event of having someone over to your house for dinner, stage and set the landscape of your waking life in preparation of reception. Notice what that evokes within you. Notice how you begin to move and see in that preparatory state of being. Notice what that communicates to your conscious mind and how you feel in your body. And recognize how such activity of preparation also amplifies your resonance in the Field. Taking action from this level of alignment loudly communicates your readiness and willingness to receive the patterns or events you are preparing for.

There is a tendency, possibly unconscious, to put off preparation for a later time. A tendency in which you might say "Oh I'll do that when the time comes" which suggests that you in your own mind are holding to the notion that the time is not right now. Instead of getting ready, getting prepared and moving within that field of receptivity, the script runs that says the getting ready can wait until there is reason for it.

Whatever you see yourself receiving, you will receive. Things are unsure only because you set them up to be that way in your own mind. Commit to receiving the vision in your heart. Keep it alive and nourish it with acceptance, with validation, with preparation. Give it validity, reality, in your own being and prepare for it. Live in the state of being in reception of it. It is this sustained practice that turns your vision into a living experience, and the living of that experience can start now as you look at your readiness to receive and live it now.

Are you ready to receive your desired end?

Are you ready to embody it fully?

Are you ready to live it now with your whole being?

Do you already have all the things in place that you want to have in place?

Have you prepared for its arrival?

Before you step into greater success, expanding into a greater self than the self you are now will make it more congruent for you to be in that space of greater success. Often individuals will step into areas of success they are not prepared for, they will move and keep pushing into growth without creating the resonant structure of self to stand in that expanded space of "bigger" events and opportunities. No event or opportunity is actually bigger than you, for what you are is always greater than the patterns and events that show up. However, for the point of self-reference you have created and maintained, it can feel that way. So when those moments that are "bigger than the me I am right now" show up, they experience discomfort. Whatever you move toward will move toward you, the key to a resonant meeting here being that you create the internal resonance to be able to support and remain in the "bigger" spaces you move yourself toward. If an event feels too big for you, it is because you have not moved into the pattern of self that is a match to the space of that event. You have not internally prepared for it by creating the more resonant self-structure. It always comes back to resonance.

When you begin to observe your reality from the inside to the outside, you will be more than prepared to step into the opportunities that move toward you and show up before you. Before an event even shows up, the energy and changes needed within you will come through, will be visible to you – the solutions and answers will often show up before the problems or questions do. What may look like leaps or big events to others looking from the outside at you, to you will actually feel like an extension of yourself because you have already organized yourself into a pattern that supports and holds that event. The future ceases being unexpected because it is now you who is drawing it forth.

So, are you internally prepared to hold and meet your success?

Are you externally prepared to greet and house your success?

KIDEST OM

The Engine of Enthusiasm

*"Enthusiasm is a supernatural
serenity."*

- Henry David Thoreau -

There is an awareness that comes forth when you are doing something you are passionate about. When you are moving into action with excitement and enthusiasm as your sourced states of being there is a fire that burns, a sense of feeling and being a greater you, a bigger you, a more present you. A you that is flowing and pouring itself out into the task at hand. In a state of enthusiasm, of passion, of excitement, you connect and expand to be something larger than your everyday conscious awareness. You pull from a more extensive reservoir of presence, of energy, of power and you are moved by a more abundant reservoir as well.

If you take notice of the level of awareness you move through in the everyday tasks of waking reality, you will notice a sense of habituated narrow focus that just dimly lights the space around you as you move from task to task. And yet when something comes forth that engages you, this everyday awareness changes – more concentration, more focus, more absorption, more merging and fusing with whatever is at hand takes place. It is advantageous to notice this because it makes available to you the level of awareness, energy, and power, you can orient yourself toward in any given moment. Enthusiasm, passion, excitement are not states reserved for a few tasks in life. If you pay attention to the gears at work, to the internal orientation at play, you can move yourself into these states to make use of the significant momentum and vitality they breathe into whatever you focus on through them.

You can engage any state in any given moment. If your default state as you look at something in your life isn't excitement, enthusiasm, or passion, you can shift your interior consciously. You have to recognize that how you approach and from what emotion you approach any situation in your life is entirely in your control. You're not limited to your reactionary responses. You're not limited to your default learned reactions to familiar or new situations. You can infuse a current of energy that is more elevated than whatever reactionary response is arising within you. You can transcend your learned reactions in favor of more useful responses by consciously paying attention to what energy is arising within you and altering it to what you prefer or choose to be arising from you.

There is greatness within every individual that can be summoned, a vast reservoir of energy, power, and momentum that can be called to the forefront of conscious awareness and extended out into the personal field of your reality. You can rise up to any moment that faces you, you can rise up within any moment you find yourself in. Greatness has to be summoned, it will not force its way through you – you have to call it forward, you have to call it up and outward from within yourself.

What is it that drives you in those things you want to demonstrate in the world?

Are you on fire with love for the demonstration of them?

Are you on fire with love for the possession of them?

Are you on fire with love for the embodiment of them?

Is there passion behind those things you want to achieve, demonstrate, express?

Do you recognize that if they are not yet expressed from the states of passion and excitement, that they can be?

There is something noticeable that happens to the very spin of your personal matrix when you are consumed with the passion to bring something into being. It has heat. It has increased velocity, a palpable feel, and vibrancy that fills up the field of your awareness. It crackles and sparks like the sound of two sticks hitting before they ignite into fire. And the very focus of your being has a driven direction, a fuelled expulsion that is moving you into the very experiences sought in your heart.

When you are passionate, excited, and enthused by something, you are in a way consumed by it. To be consumed by something means to be absorbed, ingested, and digested by that something. The very space and field of this something, the very energies of this something consume you as you consume it. Let the electricity of your success consume you, ingest you, digest you. Let it absorb you into itself. Let the magnetic reality of your success and fulfilment, of the events that reflect your success and fulfilment, take over you. Let it light and drive you.

The state of transmuting one thing into another, the process of your transformation from one pattern of self into another, one world into another, can have this alchemical quality to it that you can experience as you move yourself into states of enthusiasm to ignite the evolutionary leap of self you are setting into motion. Are you excited, energized, enthused by the field of your success? What happens to you in these states? What happens to the voltage of your cells? What happens to the spin and velocity of your personal energy field? What happens when you use the engine of enthusiasm for popping yourself into new fields of experience?

What happens then?

What do you feel then?

I am driven by the energy of my success.

I am lived by the vitality of my fulfilment in this moment and in every moment.

I am consuming and being consumed by the resonant field of my success.

I am success, and success is me.

Eagerness, enjoyment, excitement are all indicators of energy moving in a free and abundant manner through the nervous system. Enthusiasm is both a mobilizing force and an indicator of momentum in the creative flow of experience – it is fuel, and it is fire. To be enthusiastic for your success, to be enthusiastic about your fulfilment, to be enthusiastic about yourself and about life, is to allow the core creative energy of the Universe to freely circulate and flow within and through your entire being, and out into your world.

Whatever energy or resonance you are

holding yourself in, relating to something, is a resonance that reaches out and expresses itself through and as that something. Circumstances and conditions don't need to change if they don't carry a sense of aliveness for you. It is your own resonance that has to change. You are what you infuse into the world around you. You are what you project onto the Universal screen space of waking reality. It's always about you, what you are drawing from, what you are flowing from, what you are allowing to move through you and as you into the world.

The very fibre of existence, of your being, of the Field or Universe, is this excited, excitable, endlessly vibrant field of dancing energy. It is alive. It is vibrating, and that ceaseless vibration is akin to what you experience when you are feeling passion, eagerness, enthusiasm, and excitement. How you feel in these states, reflect the essence of the ocean of particles forming you and your world. It is this Infinite aliveness that creates everything around you.

Everything in creation is saying: I'm so excited I could just scream.

This Infinite aliveness of the Universe, this aliveness of your animated world and being is always present, is always here. Whether or not you are awake to it and experiencing it, experiencing the energized vitality of everything in you and around you, is about the mind and lens you are using to register and experience it. Looking at something through the lens of eagerness and enjoyment allows that something to be seen in that same energy of eagerness and enjoyment. Excitement births more excitement. Eagerness births more eagerness. Enthusiasm births more enthusiasm. Passion births more passion. You do not see the world as it really is. You see the world as you yourself are. So as you attune yourself to states of passion, you will see that passion that is inherent in everything. As you attune yourself to states of excitement, you will awaken to the excitement in everything.

Feel into these states and notice how they open you up. Feel into what it's like to be excited about something. Your whole entire being becomes electrified. Your whole entire being becomes energized, you can feel the inner vibration of the life that forms you and your world. Everything feels more open, electric, and alert. Everything about you feels fully alive. It's the same when you feel enthusiasm for something or toward something – it's as if you are overtaken by a different kind of energy, one that is more vibrant, more energizing, more animating, more alert and awake.

How excited are you for your success?

How excited are you for your fulfilment?

How enthusiastic are you about your fulfilment?

How eager are you for your success?

As you are eager for success, then success is eager for you. As you are excited about your success, then your success is excited for you. One continuous field – all ways and always.

One of the easiest ways to get back into the electrified flow of an enthused awareness is the practice of gratitude. What you experience as eagerness and enthusiasm, excitement and joy, is a range of frequencies or a state of being that you can access easily by focusing on the blessings already in your world. Through gratitude, through thankfulness, through noticing the wonder and gifts of your world as it appears right now, you accelerate the energy field of your heart and mind. In doing this, you access the states you feel as enthusiasm, aliveness, passion, and eagerness. If you don't already practice gratitude, start. It's not only a useful practice but also a powerful and easy access point to your expansion. Daily move yourself into accessing states that are supportive of Consciousness expansions and the generation of more resonant patterns of self through gratitude.

The dulling of perception, the stagnation or congestion of your flow, comes about because you normalize the miracles and gifts that have already come into view in your personal reality. You gloss over them in your mind and begin to see them as faded background props in your waking experience. Everything is new right now, however. Even the things that have been in your sight and in your life for what you perceive to be "a very long time" are entirely new in this moment carrying with them an ever-renewing essence of excited liveliness and vibrancy. And it is gratitude and the energy of appreciation that will allow you to see them in their pure light, in their eternal sparkle, and as you do you begin to resonate at a different frequency range, one that feels like excitement and enthusiasm.

This sense of eagerness, this sense of enthusiasm unlocks the flow of energy in you. Take the cap off of your flow. Turn up your thermostat of tolerance for the level of positive energy and accelerated spin that can be your baseline of being. It is the inherent excitement of life, and for life that gives you drive, that revs up your inner engines and carries you on your decided journey. All success and fulfilment, no matter its apparent grade, is laced with this undercurrent of enthusiasm and excitement. Life does not whisper itself into being, life does not tiptoe into form, it laughs and dances itself into the world of form you see all around you. The eagerness, excitement, and playfulness you see in children are pointing you to the secrets of real creative power.

Let yourself spin wildly

with the dance of light all around you.

Let yourself feel the eternal celebration
of life

that is right now the undertone

of all that you see and don't see,

in all times and spaces

across this Universe and more.

There is nothing in your way.

Being Certain of Success

What happens when success and fulfilment are your only option? What happens when all you feel is a complete unequivocal and unwavering commitment to your desired ends? What happens when you move into knowing with every fibre of your being that success and fulfilment are yours at every turn? When you move into such a state, the reality of your success and fulfilment extends itself as a solid ground before you. It all becomes very concrete and dense enough that it feels like you can touch it and skip right across it.

Before you even begin to witness the reality of your desired end, you can move yourself into a state of certainty. Certainty is a state of being. It's a feeling you can access and anchor in mind, heart and body. It's an internal conviction that cannot be influenced or swayed by input from your external world, whether from people or circumstances. When you are sure of your fulfilment, what other's think, say or do won't matter to you. When you are internally convinced of your success, you will be unmoveable by the currents of circumstances that organize and dissolve all around you. You will broadcast a constant and clear signal into the Field, you will become a clear and unceasing magnetic song in the Universe, to beckon forward the very desired outcomes you had become certain of. The realization to anchor within yourself is that there is nothing and no one in the world that can stop you from feeling your certainty.

Certainty is a powerful state of being to leverage in any endeavor, in any point of focus. A state of certainty grounds you and locks you into the field of your desired end. Certainty is stable, assured, doubtless, clear, firm. It plants itself in any field and remains unmoved in its ways. A lighthouse, a statue, a deeply rooted pillar – this is the sense a state of certainty evokes in you. It taps into an inner power, an inner authority, an internal feeling of command and it is a useful pattern to move into and have move into you when it comes to organizing your reality in a way that expresses the desires of your heart.

There is a certain degree of focus and direction, a sense of purposefulness that comes along with the state of certainty. It has an energetic structure, psychological anatomy that expresses itself in your physiology. This is something you can observe directly. When you are uncertain about things, your focus is scattered, your mind is clouded, your body has points of tension all throughout. Cloudiness, fuzziness, confusion, insecurity, instability are all varied expressions of the uncertain state. The moment you shift yourself into a state of certainty, your posture changes, your attitude changes, the way you look out onto the world changes, the way you breathe changes, the way you walk changes, what fills your mind changes, and what and how you see out into the world changes. In certainty, you are clearer, more defined, more coherent, and radiate a sense of stability and presence that is hidden in states of uncertainty. In certainty you are the very focusing of the force of creation. Such a noticeable physical change points to what the state of certainty connects you to and allows you to organize as. You have the power and ability to be a commanding presence, a focused beam and presence of creative power, and it is in a state of certainty you know that the world about you is secondary to the being-ness that you are. Because it is.

If you were to right now fully know that you are a powerful creative being of limitless resources, what level of certainty would you access when it comes to your experience of success?

Look at where that question takes you. Look and feel into how you relate to the energy of success when you are in a state of certainty about who and what you are, and what you can access in any given moment. If you are an integrated point of Consciousness in a field of Infinite Potential, then what you know of yourself and the field around you informs how you show up in your moments, in your world. A state of certainty moves you into the assumption of your own power as a creative presence in the world. How much creative power you access and how much creative power you allow is tied to how certain you are about what you can do in the world, who you can be in the world, what you can express in the world. And let's make a deeper insertion here about your nature – it isn't that you have creative power, it is that you are creative power. It isn't that you have force or presence, it is that you are force and presence. The very essence that organizes itself as you is power, is force, is presence. And it is the states you move into that reveals just how limitless this power, force, and presence that you are really is.

I am certain.

I am assured.

I am planted firmly in the field of my success.

You can be certain of the desired end, of your inevitable success, while remaining curious, flexible, and open to the way in which that desired end comes into formation. This is an important distinction to make. Being rigid in how your reality organizes isn't useful, it makes you unavailable to means and systems beyond your limited conscious parameters to come through. Being certain in the possibility that your reality can reorganize in a desired way however is very useful.

NOTHING IN THE WAY

Notice the difference between knowing that your success is inevitable, being certain about it, and being certain you know how your success is going to come into form. There is a distinguishable difference in the sense of expansion you feel and the sense of direction you feel in these two frames of focus. When you hold yourself in a state of certainty that your success is a solid reality, everything about you is aligned, open, solid. When you hold yourself in a state of certainty over how your success will come into form, when you create a sense of knowing the details of your success, there's a mental contraction that happens as you try to hold in your mind all the details necessary to form the finished product of your success. There is much more detail than you can consciously hold, and so naturally you contract as you move into your version of how things happen to the exclusion of the infinite unknown pathways the Field can organize. So moving into a state of certainty about your fulfilment while remaining open as to how your fulfilment will come into visibility focuses your being outside the field of your conscious limits.

This makes you both pointed and receptive, both focused in a specific direction and boundless to the flow of materialization; it combines the complementary gears of your creative mechanism, the electric and magnetic systems within you and around you. In your certainty of the principles of creation, in your certainty of your true identity, you will celebrate the fulfilment and success of your desired end before you see any evidence of it. You come into knowing that is beyond the realms of conscious sensory based knowledge.

How solid are you in your knowing of Consciousness as the sole cause of your experience?

How certain and sure are you of the fulfilment of your every desire?

Certainty emerges out of the premises you have rooted yourself into. You either hold Consciousness to be the primary cause or you on some level subscribe to the notion that there are external factors that you have to weigh in, include, make space for in your perceptual field of awareness. Either your desire has already been met, accomplished, formed in perfection in the field of infinite potentiality, or there are obstacles, limitations, problems in the way of it because it isn't yet created or finished or really there. Or either your desire is already a complete pattern in the Field, or it is something you have to make happen, that you have to chisel, and push, and fight to bring into being. These are just a few of the perceptual templates you hold or could be working from, and so you want to look at them before you start looking out from and through them.

NOTHING IN THE WAY

When you ask, is it already given?

When you wish, is it already fulfilled?

Is the creative field of the Universe an empty canvas?

Is your desire an echo of patterns that are already complete in the Field?

Notice the foundational premises you are pulling from to construct your experience of waking reality. The reality of your desired end precedes its appearance. That it is true, that it is a living reality, that it is already accomplished is a fact before you even begin to tune into it with your conscious awareness. There is actually nothing in the way of your success, your fulfilment, your desired end. It is there before you even go looking for it as all possible patterns already exist in the Intelligent Field that forms itself as this you and this world. Just as there are endless locations on a map that you may or may not be aware of, there are countless realities that are unfolding in complete perfection and form in the Unified creative field. Your desired end, your success, your fulfilment is given before you even think to ask for it. It is not something that is going to take place in the distance, in the future, in a different point in time and space. It is a solid living ground you can bring yourself to stand on by accessing the states of being that correspond with the completed pattern. Within the Field of Infinite Possibilities, are Infinite Realities that are perfect and complete, and that you have access and the capacity to tune into at any given moment.

Whatever desired end you want, whatever preferred outcome you want is already present in perfect and complete form. The friendships, relationships, career outcomes, state of health or wealth you desire is a perfect and complete pattern of resonance that exists right here and now. You don't have to create it, you only have to become attuned to it, or put another way, you only have to change the angle of reference you are using to see it and live it.

Can you hold to the pattern of your fulfilment and success without wavering?

Can you allow yourself to be certain of the perfect fulfilment that is already looking at you and ready to look through you?

Whatever appears, whatever manifests along the way, remain in your certainty of fulfilment. Never be swayed by the apparent experience of there being no movement on your path to success and fulfilment. Where things don't appear to be moving are exactly the moments in which a great deal is unfolding. Remain in your certainty. Change seems to come in spurts and yet change is the base reality of every part of waking life. Even now, there are unaccountable changes happening within you and around you, all under the surface of your conscious awareness. Even when it doesn't look to be so to your limited sensory registers, there is so much change, so much movement, so much creative orchestration taking place in every avenue of your experience. Your knowledge of this will allow you to notice the threads of change that are weaving new worlds of experiences for you.

You want to move into the knowing that no movement, no progress, no change are illusions only manufactured by the conscious mind's need to create stability and familiarity. Hidden beneath your conscious mind's tendency to average out signals in the Field into familiar patterns, is endless and continuous information on the changes taking place in every direction of your waking life. Remain certain of your fulfilment. Change is the norm. Difference is the order of every moment. And so those moments on the path where it appears that nothing is happening, are precisely the moments in which a great deal of activity is taking place. These are the moments you want to celebrate, that you want to be ecstatic about – when all appears to be still, when nothing seems to be happening, pop open the cork of celebration for in these moments forces beyond your conscious awareness are collaborating and colliding your success into form.

When you get on your path, stay on it, knowing with all parts of yourself that change is what's filling up every single step that you take. Stay the course, and never be fooled by the appearance of no change. Never be deceived by the illusion of sameness, by the mirage of no change. Nothing is as it was a moment ago. No part of your life is as it was a moment ago. It is already different and changing still. Let yourself solidify in the knowing that the change that is continually unfolding through you and around you will be in the direction of your desired end if you are keeping yourself in that state of certainty, harmony, congruence, and resonance with the field of your desired fulfilment. Be sure of your full success. Be certain of your total fulfilment. There is nothing in your way.

Your Success Is Complete

Consciousness is whole and complete. Its completion precedes all things. Whenever you desire something, whenever you feel the desire to experience something, that desire is reflecting something already accomplished in Consciousness. All manifestation is the projection of something already finished in the non-local Field of Consciousness. Every outcome is something that already exists in full completed form in the inner realms of creation.

Your success is already accomplished; its accomplishment precedes your desire for it. Your success and the means and the paths for it is already a fully formed whole pattern in the psyche of Cosmic Intelligence. All parts of it are mapped out, its full potential already coded and expressed into a complete image for you to bring into materialization. It is the same continuum of fulfilment and wholeness that you experience as desire and the manifestation of what's desired. It is the same creative thread of life unbroken and complete from one end of desire to the other end of fulfilment. In the same way conscious awareness of the decision to act actually is recognized or experienced after the act has occurred, awareness of a desire arises after the fulfilment of the desire has formed. This is a useful analogy to consider as you look at the experiences of success and fulfilment you are desiring or intending to draw into your life.

If you can right now recognize your desire for some end as the aftermath of an event that has already occurred in the Field of Infinite Potentiality, how do you now relate to this desire?

If you were to right now recognize that the desired success is a complete and total reality reaching back to meet you, what would you notice?

All that you are looking at as evidence for your success is a reflection of all that was already finished within your being. Nothing out there actually is independent of your being – it is all reflecting and echoing patterns you have already lived inside of you, in realms beyond time and space. You as Consciousness are already in the end of what you desire to experience, you get there before your physical reality does. You go there and dwell in the space of your success and fulfilment before your conscious mind, your body, your environment reflects the "reality" of that. The spaces you visit in waking experiences are spaces you have already occupied in the hidden dimensions of Consciousness. As within, so without. This is always the flow of manifestation, from the inside to the outside, from the invisible to the visible, from Consciousness into the world of matter.

I am awake to the primacy of Consciousness.

I am awake to the first cause of my experience.

I am awake to my guaranteed fulfilment.

I am awake to what I desire already being so.

How can anything ever be in the way, when you are already there? What you come to live, what you come to face is the spaces of Consciousness you have already lived in in the subtler realms or octaves of being. What is new to your conscious mind, what is new to your eyes, are the distances you have already travelled in the inner recesses of your being. Consciousness has already gone before you to prepare all that you come to live. It has arranged the stage, it has dotted every "I" and crossed every "t" long before you consciously began to seek out some preferred outcome.

Consciousness comes first. It came first. It went first. This is the recognition that will allow you to experience the creative power that extends itself into the world as a physical you. The spaces and locations accessed within your own being, the energies accessed within, are always what come to face you on the screen space of your reality. This is the constant awareness that will save you from questioning, doubting, or wondering. This is the steady awareness you want to cultivate. It is what will reveal to you the immense power inside of you that is expressing as you. The creative nature of who and what you really are is unfathomable to the conscious mind. But how does Consciousness do that? How is that even possible? Such a response or reaction is born of the assumption that linear time is real and that things unfold sequentially, in a logical order. In the realms of Consciousness, no such rules exist. All patterns, all paths, all possibilities freely float and dance conforming to a science that is beyond linear understanding.

Are you willing to entertain the possibility that your desired success, your desired fulfilment, whatever end you desire, is an already established complete pattern in the Field?

Does the unfolding of events need to conform to your linear understanding of time and logical sequence?

Can Consciousness operate and unfold itself in ways beyond your current physical understanding of what waking experience is?

NOTHING IN THE WAY

If you know, and can bring yourself to know, that Consciousness precedes all manifestation, the Consciousness that you are comes before, prior to all that you see, then it is not the manifestation you bow to but the Consciousness that you are, the Consciousness that comes before all things. This is as close to Grace as you can live inside yourself. Form, matter, or circumstances, are secondary – they are the reflection in the mirror you are standing in front of. They are how Consciousness comes to know itself through the lens of the spaces it has gone to reside in.

Where you get sidetracked is when you take your eyes off of this primacy of Consciousness and tell yourself that the manifestation is something that's happening outside of you, apart from you, separate from you. When it's really not. Letting manifestation lead you, inform you, instead of going inward and being informed by this Greater presence is momentously cheating yourself. Manifestation is the extension of your own body, the body of Consciousness as it is being expressed as this unique you. Always remember Consciousness as the sure and certain cause of all that takes shape before you and you will find yourself detaching from any pattern of resistance and any reliance on the formed world to direct and lead you. When you bow only to this primacy of Consciousness, you are lead, guided, and directed by a power, presence, and intelligence residing beyond the confines of time, space, and human constructs and rules.

As you move about your world in waking reality, you are either magnifying manifestation, or you are magnifying the power and primacy of Consciousness. Although these are ultimately one and the same, when you look to the effect as the power, you are turning your attention away from the one and only true power, source, and resource in this experience. This is where insecurity, fear, doubt come in. Only when you have turned away from the power of Consciousness, do you find yourself in doubt or uncertainty. If you can see through all matter and see the Consciousness that has extended itself as all patterns, then you are already ahead of the game. If you can see through the veil of all appearances and recognize the living unified power at back of all things, you are already in the true creative seat that is set up for you. Whatever the desired end, know that it is already so.

Nothing Is In the Way

Success is yours.

Fulfilment is yours.

Happiness is yours.

Whatever success you are looking to experience is not behind some obstacle you have to overcome. Obstacles are perceptual limits created in the mind and upheld in the mind. What you interpret as an obstacle and what you interpret as a support mechanism or manifestation is free-floating information you are confining to the limit or boundary of "bad thing". Nothing is what you think it is outside of your thoughts, outside of your definitions. The moment you release all definitions and constructs from your awareness, you will see firsthand that nothing in the world around you has any meaning built into it. In this recognition, you can re-define anything that shows up to mean something different. Changing the meaning you give any specific thing is changing the energy you allow yourself to experience as it relates to that thing. Question the meanings you impose on the events around you. Question the definitions you plaster onto the situations and circumstances of your current reality. Manage the quality of energy you are feeding yourself and resonating with consciously, and you'll directly experience your power to flatten apparent mountains in your view. Nothing in front of you actually means what you think and feel it means. Your interpretations are your creative lens informing, distorting and altering your experience of yourself, relationships and world.

Obstacles are not obstacles – they are neutral appearances onto which the definition and concept, and so command expression of obstacle-ness are being applied to. That bears repeating – obstacles are not obstacles. There is actually no such thing as an obstacle apart from the creative sound barrier you create around a pattern through the construct "obstacle". If you tell a pattern that it is an obstacle with heart and conviction, it will behave like one. Let yourself recognize and awaken to the constructs, the structures of Consciousness, you employ to form your world. Challenges, obstacles, difficulty, hardships are all conceptual brackets you make use of to mold and shape how you experience the flow of neutral and meaningless information.

Be willing to ask yourself: *what am I making this mean? Is this meaning useful?*

The mind that perceives an obstacle is itself the obstacle. Stop perceiving walls and blocks where there are none and realize that every obstacle is self-manufactured, self-created, and perceived by the very mind that is affirming its imagined existence. If you perceive obstacles, if you perceive walls, it is because you are building them and maintaining them in your own mind. If you look within yourself, you will see the constructs, concepts, definitions, assumptions that are projecting the apparent barrier. The creative Field you are looking out onto, the intelligent Field that surrounds you is not at all one that is defined, fragmented, and separated into "obstacles" and "clear paths". A Unified Field is one that is without any formations, nothing is this or that. And yet as a creative presence, you can form boundaries where there are none. You have the internal creative technology, through the use of sound (words, definitions, assumptions) to create the illusion of things being there. What is it that informs your definition of an obstacle? How do you know that what you are looking at is this thing that is defined as such? When did you first become aware of things being obstacles?

You want to look at the beliefs you are keeping active. You want to examine the thoughts you are holding as truths and true measures of the way things are in the world. You want to look at the creative tools you are employing in your waking experience. You want to move yourself into the realization that all that you perceive as possible and not possible is perception and perception only, and that recognition alone is powerful. Perception can be changed, altered, modified, in the blink of an eye. Meaning can be altered, modified, discarded. Parameters can change, be adjusted, or removed altogether. And so all that you see before you, around you, and all that you notice within you is malleable.

Clear the way in your own mind, drop the thoughts that are making excuses, drop the thoughts that are implying or suggesting that things are in the way, or can be in the way, and *what do you notice*? What is actually there without the sound current of pattern-defining narrative that is running?

What if there was nothing in the way of your success right now?

What if you were right now standing in the middle of your fulfilment? How do you know that you are not?

Notice the feeling, the energy, the sense all around you as you drop the limitations you were holding up in your own mind. Look into and with the undifferentiated awareness that has no conditions. Move this awareness around your fields of experience and look again. You are not able to move into the space of your fulfilment only when you are fabricating and upholding reasons not to enter it. What's in the way is not really in the way. What's in the way is an externalization of a perceptual limit you allowed to go unchecked. You've heard of the saying to look fear right in the face to see what it's made of. Look again at whatever appears to be an obstacle in this same way. Really look at it. What is it made of? What about it is in your way? Outside of your insistence that it's in the way, outside of that psycho-emotional projection "this is in the way" that you are extending out from yourself and looking through, is there really anything in the way? Really look closely at it. And then look at it again from an undifferentiated space of being – from the clear space of awareness that isn't masked by any thoughts, beliefs, definitions, labels. Without thoughts, emotions, definitions, beliefs, labels about whatever it is you are looking at, what's there?

What holds you back from your success is...you. Movement, motion, momentum are contained in the patterns you are en-training yourself with. Out of an infinite number of patterns available to you, what is it that is making you gravitate toward patterns that are about not entering the field of your desired outcome?

You want to let yourself live in the realization that whatever success you see about you, whatever level of fulfilment you desire, whatever level of satisfaction your heart craves through some expression or manifestation, is already a living reality for you. The Universe holds nothing back from you, for in an Undifferentiated Ocean of Consciousness there is nothing that is denied or can be denied. Denial exists only in one place, within the constructs you have made real within yourself, and within the experiential boundaries you've assumed to be possible for you.

WHATEVER THIS CREATIVE INTELLIGENT FIELD HAS MADE AVAILABLE TO OTHER'S, IS AND WILL ALWAYS BE AVAILABLE TO YOU IN LIMITLESS FORM.

Feel yourself into this re-tuning: *whatever walls and obstacles I perceive before me now show themselves to only be a simulation of my own mind. Nothing is in my way. My way is clear and lighted with the limitless light of this Intelligent Universe.*

"When you are inspired by some great purpose, some extraordinary project,

all your thoughts break their bonds:

Your mind transcends limitations,

your Consciousness expands in every direction,

and you find yourself in a new, great and wonderful

NOTHING IN THE WAY

world.

Dormant forces, faculties and talents become alive,
and you discover yourself to be

a greater person by far

than you ever dreamed yourself to be."

— Patanjali

Nothing is in the way. Nothing is in your way.

KIDEST OM

NOTHING IN THE WAY

Owning Your Fulfilment

What you desire to be fulfilled by is yours, your birthright, your inheritance, your gift from the very Universe that formed you and forms you right now. It is the gift of your Self, and it is a gift that has no cost or exchange value. You are gifted total fulfilment simply because you exist. Change can happen in the blink of an eye. Fulfilment can arise in the very next breath or even in the middle of this one. You don't have to earn or labour for the changes you desire. You don't have to exert yourself to exhaustion to reach the summit of your highest and best experience. You did not have to fashion the earth and the sun yourself, you did not have to mold the physical body and its entire organ system yourself, you did not have to pave every inch of the ground you walk on yourself. As much as you are a participator of your world, you are also in large part a receiver of the flow of the Intelligence that has formed itself as everything that is you and everything that is your world right now.

One of the patterns you must break on your success journey is the belief pattern that your worth is determined by how hard you work or how much you produce or how other people perceive you. Hard work, levels of productivity, and other people's evaluation of you are all informed by belief patterns that are contained within the only determining factor of your worthiness. All of these conditions on your worth and what makes you worthy are superfluous. The only deciding factor of your worth and how you experience your worth is your own Consciousness. Nothing else actually decides how worthy you are. No one else actually dictates how worthy you are. Your value, your worth, your deserve-ability are only ever limited by your own constructs around your worthiness. When you clearly establish yourself in this understanding that you have immense worth just as you are, there's not a thing anyone can say or do and not a thing any situation can imply that will touch or alter your realization of your enormous value.

Nothing is actually in the way of your total fulfilment. Nothing is actually in the way of your highest experiences of fulfilment. It is when you realize that nothing is in the way that you come to live that nothing is in the way. When you realize the state of it being a clear and unobstructed path for you, when you live in the space of this realization, you will live this in your waking world. Your fulfilment is as near as your own mind allows it to be, it is as present and in reach as you can accept it to be within yourself. For always, as within your own mind, so it is reflected in your waking world. You're already worthy. You're already valuable. You're already deserving. You're already capable. You're already a living genius. You're already enough. Let yourself notice all the ways in which this is already true and expand that awareness. Wake up to it and wake up within it in every direction of your life.

The more you are awake to your present fulfilment, the more your present fulfilment wakes up in you. It is already inside of you. Look at how you are already successful. Look through the eyes of the success you have already brought into form, that has formed itself through you. Look at the brilliance of the body you make use of. Look at the brilliance of the mind that receives, filters, includes or excludes information. Extend your awareness out into your experiences and notice where you are already living success.

TIP: *Noticing Where You Have Succeeded*

In the constant plight for foreword movement and progression, the conscious mind quickly filters out where you have already brought about desired outcomes. The forward-looking mind is useful in that it keeps your momentum going. It is also useful however, to stop and allow yourself to really take notice of how you've already brought about so many desired ends into your experience. Every success, every win, every fulfilment you have ever experienced came about through you and from you. Own this recognition. Even when you took yourself to be a passive participant and a passive recipient of the life you are living, you were still a masterful and magnetic creative power. Whatever your area of focus, acknowledging where you have been already successful and how you have already been fulfilled will expand your focus and add fuel to your current momentum. This effortless shift or reorientation will allow you to notice more of your ongoing state of fulfilment.

Take a moment to notice regularly where you have succeeded and what that looked and felt like. Pencil it in as a mental workout on your calendar. If there is one specific area where you want more growth and success, then notice what's already at the back of that. Create a success tree and add the leaves of what's already shown up in support of this desired end. With this awareness, you will continue to move into it as a growth of what's already forming rather than as something new you have to bring through. The conscious mind can be good at forgetting the miraculous moments that have already shaped themselves all around you and so a little nudge into remembering what's already proven itself as possible to you is sometimes necessary.

What this will allow you to move into is the recognition of possibility in the areas you now want to grow, shift, adjust, or manifest different outcomes altogether.

There is no obstacle to the change you want.

There is no obstacle to the relationship you want.

NOTHING IN THE WAY

There is no obstacle to the home you want

There is no obstacle to the promotion you want.

There is no obstacle to the raise you want.

There is no obstacle to the career you want.

There is no obstacle to any face of success you desire.

Success and fulfilment are present states of being you can pre-assume. Because Consciousness can move into any field, you can right now, in this moment, drop all else and reside or occupy the feeling space of already being fulfilled. Nothing stops you from moving into the spatial location of your desired end – the movement in Consciousness like that can only be interfered with by your unwillingness to psychically or psychologically "go there" now. You can make present the state you would experience were the desired end already here.

As you achieve the realization of fulfilment within yourself right here and now in this way, no external appearance can move or sway you. When you let yourself source from this space of fulfilment, you come to know that what you desire is yours, that it is already granted and given to you, and the contradictions in your being cease and so the contradictions in your outer world dissolve. You reach a state of immovability within yourself – no appearance disturbs you for you are in the knowing of your present fulfilment.

States have a way of solidifying into reality. At first, when you move into such a state of feeling, such a space of Consciousness without manifested cause, it may feel like you're trying out foreign equipment where the instructions in the manual are written in a language you can't read. And yet as you continue to reside in the state and harmonize with it, it comes to feel natural. This isn't a process that takes months or years. In most cases, depending on the level of resistance you have built up, you can achieve full harmonization within minutes to a few days at most.

As you acclimate to the resonance, no other information matters. No other appearance is of consequence. You are steady and stable in your realization of your fulfilment. You are certain in your realization that what you wish for most in your heart is already gifted to you regardless of whether this is visible to your physical senses as yet. Faith, acceptance, reception, trust, are all the mechanics of this inner stability, they are states of mind, states of being, fields of resonances that rely and lean upon the invisible 99.9% of reality as the source and resource of all fulfilment. In this state of knowing, you simply know what you know.

NOTHING IN THE WAY

Are you a match to this: It's too good to not be true, too wonderful not to happen, too good not to last. Long-lasting incredible happenings are the order of the day.

What's important and what matters is what has your attention. Are you attentive to your present fulfilment, or are you attentive to negating thoughts and words, patterns that deny it? You are either fuelling your journey, or you are fighting tooth and nail not to "go there". It isn't the outer world of form that matters, that's already what has materialized. The best indicator of your success is what you are harmonizing and aligning with inside of yourself. This also comes back to what you are bowing down to – are you bowing to manifestation, the dance of temporary patterns you form narratives around in your mind, or are you fully awake to the primacy and power of Consciousness? What have you made your God? For a mind that is so used to being fixated on the formed world, to begin to allow yourself to only be informed by what you don't see may require strength of focus, resolve, and commitment. And again, these are states you can call forward if needed. You always have choice.

Even science asserts that what's rich and brimming with vibrancy is the 99.9% of reality that you don't see – what appears as void, emptiness, darkness to you, is where all the possibilities and potentials of creation live. And yet, attached to and fixated on the formed visible world, you create and form a kind of devotion to the manifested world. You naively worship and believe in matter, the material, the visible temporary events and circumstances of waking life. It is powerful and useful to break and interrupt this pattern in yourself if you find you still rely on manifestation to be your guide and indicator to a degree of overlooking the true force and power of your experience. Manifestation is only temporary feedback, it is not the source or cause of your reality. Turn yourself to what you don't see with your senses, dip into the ocean of Stillness, the invisible, the Unknown. Touch the deeper realms of Consciousness often and move yourself into that middle line between the known and the Unknown. You will find more freedom and more space and flexibility there.

You have and will always have the ability to use your heart and mind in a way that supports what you desire to experience, in a way that flows with the current of your fulfilment. Your imagination, your feelings, your thoughts, your focus, your attention, your awareness – all of these are your intelligent instruments of certain fulfilment, certain success. Some people desire to be fulfilled and then begin to make pictures of a future distant moment in which they are fulfilled. Others desire success and then begin to talk about all the things that are in the way of that success. Still, others desire success and then conclude that it will happen if it's "meant" to happen relieving themselves of their creative power and handing it over to the gods of chance and happenstance. You are continually employing the creative instruments of your being in favour of or in contradiction to what you desire to experience.

Through the power of your feeling, your focus and attention, you can transform resistance into flow, tension into reception, negation into celebration. The greatest alchemical acts are performed within the inner realms of your own being. When you align and harmonize with the reality of your present success inside of your own being, you move yourself into accessing support and momentum from infinite forces that rest beyond your conscious awareness. The way you commune and communicate with all the forces of the Universe are through the states of being you make natural to yourself.

It is when you move yourself into a state of coherence, into a unified harmony of being in which you are a single eye, a single focus, a clear pattern of oscillating Consciousness in the Field, that you become both a force and powerful presence in your world. You are unstoppable in this state of being. It is this point of singularity you can move into that fills and powers you with the infinite light of the Universe.

Feel yourself into this re-tune: *I expect unexpected blessings to come to me each and every day.*

Whatever you desire, whatever you need, whatever whim or wish you have or will have, is already an existing reality in the Universal Field of creation, and it is so right now. You cannot register information that doesn't exist. You cannot want for, desire for, need for, things that have no existence. You receive, register, and project patterns that are already alive as a desire, a need, or a want. Every want you could imagine is met. Every wish you could ever stir within yourself is already fulfilled. Every need you have and will have is already provided and made available.

As you receive these words, notice the assumptions you've held on to and are holding on to. As you consider the possibility of ongoing success in the small and big steps of your life, as you imagine being lifted into success with every step and at every turn, as you imagine the Universe around you conspiring on your behalf time after time and event after event, notice the resonance you move into.

If you were to right now realize that your every need, your every present and not yet thought of future desire was already met, fulfilled, satisfied, what state do you move into?

If you were to right now realize that life, the Universe, Creation delights in your every fulfilment, what moves within you and in what direction?

Moving yourself into this realization, into this conviction will alter the way your world forms before you and around you because it alters the fabric of your own being. Anything can happen in an instant, anything can happen overnight and most often does. When you have calibrated yourself to notice this and to be aware of this, you will solidify your ability to know the spontaneous richness that forms your world. Be in awe of this creative expanse. Be in wonderment of your fulfilment. Own your creative right to be, live, and have whatever you desire. This is your rich creative playground.

How to Receive Your Outcomes

Whatever it is you desire to experience, assume that you have already received it, that it has already been given to you by the unseen forces of this creative life. One of the most receptive states you can move into is to assume you are already living the end you desire. Assuming you already have it, you already are it, you already own it, possess it and are living it internally involves you wrapping yourself, your awareness, your attention and your focus around the desired thing. The state of assuming it is already yours, whatever it is, is a state in which Consciousness merges and fuses itself with the desired end. When you assume you have that desired thing, in that assumption you have become one with it in Consciousness, you have made it a part of your energy body, you have brought the pattern and potential of that thing into your psycho-energy field.

The state of having something and the state of wanting something are noticeably different feeling-states. Feelings indicate resonance, harmonization and alignment. When you want something and continue to keep yourself in a state of wanting it, you are actually, if you look at it closely, in a state of not having it. Under the hood of "I want" are different calibrations of "I don't have". "I want this" presupposes that you don't have it yet, and through that psychological fragmentation you keep yourself separate and apart from the desired outcome. The language you use is a perfect indicator of where you are psychologically in relation to the desired outcome. Where you are saying you want something is precisely where you have erected a psychological barrier between you, as Consciousness, and the desired something as an object. This is a perceivable internal orientation you can observe within yourself. When you say to yourself that the desired outcome is already yours, however, the psychological and energetic wall between you, as subject, and the desired thing, as object, is dissolved. There is no longer any gap between you and the experience of the desired outcome. Instead of wanting the specific success and fulfilment, what happens when you are in the assumption of already having it? Feel into that internally and stay with the feeling.

If you recognize you want something, feel that you already have it, and then let go, most often this desired thing flows into your experience fluidly and effortlessly. It just shows up, and you move on with your life without a thought to how it came into your life, what it took, how it got made or anything else of the sort. It's those sustained states of wanting where you experience tension that you want to look out for and employ this mechanism of reception. Recognize what it is you desire to experience, move yourself into a clear state of already having it, being it, doing it, and then release or surrender the state of fulfilment out 360 degrees around you. Play with this process and see where it takes you. You'll receive immediate, relevant feedback from the Field when you've created resonant waves out from yourself. There's often a noticeable shift that arises within you when you've fully assumed the state of fulfilment inside yourself. There is an alignment between heart and mind, a clear sense of being one with the desired outcome that emerges into your awareness. This clear and coherent signal is what the Field registers and then echoes back to you as the desired event. Again, this isn't something that takes years to allow, minutes or days at most of feeling into your fulfilment and releasing the coherent signal out into the Field is often all that is needed.

Radios are designed to receive. They have no mechanism of denial aside from the off switch. If the radio is turned on, you can generally pick up any broadcast on the desired channel. Humans, on the other hand, have a conscious mind that frequently insists it knows the way things are in the world. It is very insistent in what it says it knows, in what it says is possible, likely, or not. Through conditioning that is reinforced by experience, you have assumptions for *how* things can happen in your world and *what* things can happen in your world. These conscious limits often act as filters that interfere with your ability to receive what you desire to experience.

When you're moving into the state of assuming

your desired end is already yours, you are
bypassing your conscious limits. Through the
simple exercise or process of feeling into your
desired outcome and aligning with it, you are letting
go of needing to use your conscious mind to map
out the "how" and "why" and "when" of your
fulfilment. The conscious mind is a useful system of
observation, but it's not the only one that you have.
There are broader mind systems active that you are
making use of to a more considerable degree than
your conscious mind. You only need to use your
conscious mind in this process to move yourself into
the states of occupying your fulfilment. Beyond that,
there is no need for it to do more. You can move
yourself into the state of assumption, the state of
assuming your fulfilment consciously at any time.
Instead of going by assumptions of limitation, that
you have either learned or unconsciously formed,
you can go by assumptions of reception.

*What would it be like if you were to right now
live in the assumption of already having what
you desire to have, already being what you
desire to be, already doing what you desire to
be doing?*

You want to move through your world while
holding yourself in the space of the assumed
fulfilment. Nothing can actually stop you from

assuming states of resonance. They are internal states you move into, mobilized by your willingness to play with them and move into them. This inner journeying of Consciousness is invisible to all else but your immediate awareness, initially. The more you hold yourself in this state of already having, being, doing, what you desire, the more you begin to be Sourced by this limitless state of fulfilment as it relates to your desired end. You start to source from your vision of a greater reality than from your perception of what has already happened. You begin to draw energy, intention, insight from the Fields of Infinite Potentiality than relying on the past, the known, the familiar.

Your state of already being fulfilled begins to inform your being, your thoughts, your emotions and your words. It begins to be the energy out of which you construct your world and self. Your world is formed out of the energy you yourself are being. When you assume reception, you assume the energy of fulfilment and that begins to be the energy out of which your world and being are formed. This sourcing from your already fulfilled state changes your energy. It changes the very spin and oscillation of your Consciousness and energy centers. It changes the quality of your energy field. It changes and enhances your magnetism. It changes you. It births you just as you birth it.

You are continually making energetic declarations to the environment that surrounds you as the living Universe. You are persistently presenting yourself, introducing yourself, to the Universe that is all around you. "Here I am, this is who I am" you continuously and silently declare. You wake up every day and declare a list of things that you are or are not. This list is running in the background announcing itself everywhere you go and wherever you don't go. If you were to make a list of all the things you know yourself to be and all the things you don't know yourself to be, you would get to preview the parameters of self out of which you are operating and originating. Are you making these self-introductions out of the state of being fulfilled, provided for, blessed? Or are you making such introductions of the state of wanting, needing, not having? These are distinctively different fields of resonances that you are offering. They are uniquely different parameters of self-ing. Different parameters of sound express as different patterns of events and circumstances.

You merge yourself with what you assume just as you merge yourself with what you consume. What you assume also assumes you. What you consume also consumes you. The mutuality of Consciousness is at work at every turn. If you assume lack, you have merged yourself to lack, you have married yourself to lack whatever its form – being it a lack of relationship, a lack of support, a lack of time, a lack of ideas, a lack of space, a lack of financial means. You are integrated with and integrated into this parameter self of lack and are manufacturing your world out of the materials of that field. If you assume fulfilment, you have merged yourself with fulfilment. You have made that your identity and state and so the field out of which you are pulling material out of as it were.

Mastering a state of receptivity, mastering a state of receiving is the art that blesses you with the whole Universe. To the receptive mind, all things are possible. To the receptive mind, all things are readily given. When you are in a state of reception, when you have assumed the state, you open yourself to simply allow without force or exertion that flow of your desired end. Force and frustration evidence resistance, evidence struggle and tension – these are states of a contracted mind, a mind that is not open to receiving. A mind that is open to receiving is naturally scanning for that reception. When you know you have a guest coming for dinner, when it's a given, you naturally and openly await their arrival. And so the receptive mind, the mind that is calibrated to receive operates in a similar open way.

Assume reception. Assuming you already have it, are it, and are doing it, completely moves you out of tension states. There is nothing to resist, no brake to step on when you are already at your destination. The vehicle is turned off and parked, and you are actually out of it stretching your legs and arms. You are at rest. When you are in the state of already having, being, doing the desired end, there is no space in your being to hold contradictory thoughts. Fear, doubt, frustration, impatience are all extensions of resistance – all tension is the expression of resistance, the expression of not only not letting yourself go **there, but also not letting yourself BE THERE.**

Resistance is how you stop yourself from merging with or marrying with your desired end. Assuming receptivity is how you become one with it so that you begin to resonate as it does. One creates tension in your being, while the other moves you into a relaxed state of completion. One supports the reality of your fulfilment while the other keeps you apart from it.

Explore:

If you were to right now fully and completely receive all that you've dreamed of and more if you were to right now have it all, how open would you be in mind and in heart?

Where in your body would you be open from?

Where in your mind would you be open from?

What would the orientation of your

Consciousness be?

Allow yourself to be in a state of reception. There are many more tools you can make use of to solidify the reality of your fulfilment. Being grateful for your fulfilment, appreciating and loving the reality of your fulfilment, taking yourself into the feeling states and reaction states of already being there, will all allow you to create and stabilize the supportive resonance that is in harmony with the field of your desired outcome. The fastest route to fulfilment is to know and live in the feeling of already being fulfilled.

Thank you for this success.

I love living this success.

I am so in love with this life.

I am so grateful for this fulfilment.

I so love all that worked together to support this.

Thank you! Thank you! Thank you!

KIDEST OM

The Secret is in the Space

"To fly as fast as thought, you must begin by knowing that you have already arrived."

- Richard Bach -

You can only be what you see yourself being, and you can only attain what you see yourself attaining. You can't do something you don't see yourself doing, and you can't fill a space you don't see yourself filling. It has to feel like a possibility for you, an option. Beyond that, the way to accelerate the realization of any end is to attain it and assume the attainment of it in your now. When you can move yourself into feeling that you are already filling the space you desire to fill, as one with the energy and vibration of it, you occupy the spatial field that the Universe then fills with the details of that fulfilment. You can attain it, assume it, consume it, occupy the space of it right now.

The space of a desired outcome, the not-yet localized or visible reality of it is a perceivable space. Just as you can feel into the space of the room you are in right now, you can feel into the space of the "room" that contains your desired outcome. Consciousness or awareness can move itself into any location, whether currently visible or not. Let yourself recognize that your desired outcome, any desired outcome, is already taking up "space" in the multidimensional field of Infinite Potential and this "space" is one that you can tune into and harmonize with at any time. It's not about the current props and players of your reality. It's not about the current narrative your environment may suggest. It's not about anything other than your ability to occupy and assume the space, the feel-able and perceivable "room" of your desired end.

Whatever reality you tune into internally, through your psycho-energetic antenna, will out-form itself into your waking experience with astounding accuracy. What you envision becomes you, and it becomes your world. And that expression or externalization of what you realize within yourself is all that unfolds as your waking world. There is something that transpires when you begin to envision some end. Since Consciousness has a quality of mutuality, when you begin to envision some end, that end, which is also Consciousness begins to envision you. You "dream" of one another. It is as though the vastness that is Consciousness begins to look at itself, begins to be aware of itself as you and as that desired end, looking, observing, and interacting with itself through these different points called "you" and the "desired outcome".

In your everyday focus, you are either seeking the absence of your desired end, or you are seeking its presence – you are looking through the lens of its absence, or you are looking from the lens of its presence. You are either saying "this thing I desire is here and unfolding brilliantly" or you are saying "this thing that I desire isn't here, something other than what I want is unfolding right now". The lens you are looking through, and the reality you are experiencing are one and the same. There is no actual separation of self and world, of mind and outcome. But through the perceived separation you create the experience of there being something "other" to seek "out there" in the separate and independent world. With your attention, you are giving focus to one side of the coin. When you are noticing all the ways in which it isn't visible, you are actively seeking its absence. When you are noticing all the ways in which it is present, solid, real, you are actively seeking its presence. It is all about your attention and at what angle you have positioned it.

Be willing to ask yourself: *which side of the coin am I actively seeking?*

All possibilities are both there and not there. All potentialities are both present and not present, here and not here. It is your own awareness of them or your own observation of them that makes one the reality and not the other. Focusing on the absence of the desired end, actively looking for how it isn't here, how it's not going to work out, how there are things in the way, throws you into states of resistance. You contract. You feel off centre or out of the flow. You start projecting more of the absence of your desired end into the next moment, into the future and wrap yourself into knots trying to figure out how you're going to someday get to fix or change the situation to be what you want it to be. You start by negating your fulfilment and extend that negation out in front of you as your inevitable reality, your inevitable future. Contraction is as creative as expansion – meaning what you flow from yourself from a state of contraction will bring you more things to feel contracted about. Creation never ceases.

It in no way serves you to move about your moments through states of resistance. Tension states, states of lack, incompleteness, failure, states of being that weigh you down, or decrease the velocity of your energy field go against the natural weightlessness of your being. These are states that perceptively move you away from your desired end, they spin you in the opposite direction of where you want to end up.

My fulfilment is cosmically supported.

My success is guaranteed.

My success is accomplished.

My fulfilment is a solid reality.

NOTHING IN THE WAY

My fulfilment is already given to me.

An avalanche of success and fulfilment is mine.

I am flooded with waves and waves of success and fulfilment every day.

Say to yourself: *I now let go of all resistance to my fulfilment. I now stop holding myself apart from the reality of already being fulfilled now, already being in my full success now.*

Feel yourself into this space and sustain the feeling. Move into it again and again. Mine the feeling until it saturates your whole entire being.

I now let go of all resistance to my success. I now stop holding myself apart from the reality of my full success right now.

If you were to right now already have the desired success, what would you feel?

Notice that. In Consciousness, the state can precede the manifestation, and in fact always does though it is not within your conscious awareness. Social conditioning has created the tendency to wait to move into states until after manifestation.

Ordinarily, the expectation is that manifestation determines state of being. The story goes "I will feel happy when I have accomplished this" instead of "I will accomplish this because I am already happy." The true source of any manifestation is the assumed state of Consciousness that upholds all appearances in the outer world of waking experience. A state of Consciousness is a location of space you move your identity or point of reference into. In the Fields of Consciousness are many mansions in which to move into and explore. The secret is in occupying the space of your fulfilment, a location in the nonlocal Field that you translate as a state of being.

The creative freedom you are endowed with is this, it is that Consciousness can assume any space regardless of what seems to be the reality of the moment. The reality of the moment can change in the blink of an eye, and yet it is this same reality that is perpetuated in waiting for something else to come and replace it. You don't have to wait to assume the feeling of success in any endeavor. The power is not in the manifestation. The power is always in the Consciousness, the assumed states, that is at back of the manifestation.

The state you experience when something appears is a state that has always been there, a mansion of experience that's always existed, only you give yourself permission to tune into it, move yourself and locate yourself into it, and source from it only after the formation of some event or circumstance. You don't have to wait to feel into the space of your desired outcome, to locate or re-locate your Consciousness "there" and begin to look out from it right now. Such an unconditional re-location changes your relationship to everything around you, and you will directly experience the power and freedom that has always been inside of you.

I am already successful in all the ways I want to demonstrate.

I am already fulfilled in unimaginable ways.

I assume, attain, and consume the reality of my fulfilment now.

Move yourself into the feeling space of your desired end. Again and again, bring yourself to feel that you already have it, you already are it, you already are doing it. Occupy this space of feeling, assume this state of being and witness as your world reorganizes itself in response to your relocating your Consciousness into the Field of your desired outcome.

KIDEST OM

The Art of Letting Go

Do you trust yourself? Do you trust your creative power? Do you trust the broader Field, the Universe, this creative platform that makes up your waking world? Do you include the Cosmos, Infinite Intelligence in your reality creation efforts? Do you trust in your ability to consciously interact with and influence the living Matrix that continuously forms itself all around you and through you? You have to not only trust the paths of manifestation and be comfortable in not knowing the "how" of your journey you also must bring yourself to trust your own creative nature and the broader interconnected Field at large. This ability to trust is a crucial cornerstone in your creative mastery. Trust is a very useful pillar to lean on for any creative point of Consciousness. At the root of the experience and expression of trust are solid assumptions that hold: the Universe is safe; the Universe loves me; I am supported; I am guided; I am creative; I am powerful; this serves me, this is a resource; I am always connected; I am always heard, felt, held; I am whole, unified, One.

The paths to fulfilment are many and beyond the capacity of the reasoning conscious mind to map out. The means, the way, the "how" of how things come to pass is something you have to bring yourself to surrender, to give up, to let go of – in total trust. Abandon the need to control manifestation. Release the need to dominate, manipulate or force your environment to conform to your vision. The moment you try to figure it out, the moment you try to make the "how" fit into your version of how things happen and how things can happen, the moment you try to control or force your outcome into form, you suffocate the very flow of manifestation. Trust. Let go. Release the need to control, dictate, figure out the means that a greater Consciousness itself orchestrates. This is a key practice to engage because your ego-mind or ego-self will usually very much want to stick its psychological fingers into every aspect of the manifestation process.

The capacity of the three-dimensional mind is useful in clarifying the desired end. The mechanisms of the heart and mind together are powerfully useful in allowing you to access the Field of the desired end and begin your dance of resonance with it. But how the contents of fulfilment manifest are ordered by a higher seeing, a level of Consciousness or mind that is beyond the three-dimensional worldview of your everyday mind. A greater intelligence that sees more, knows more, and orchestrates in a unified and multi-angled way is what shapes the means and the way of your fulfilment. This is what laces the journey with wonder, magic, and awe. This is where the Alice-in-Wonderland deep into many rabbit holes experience unfolds itself all around you. What sources you is a power that will always appear surreal, supernatural, and otherworldly to your conscious mind when you just let go. And so you want to consciously bring yourself to let go into that, to dissolve yourself in the ocean of possibilities for how your desired ends can come to pass. Trust that greater power and be moved from that place of trust. The wonder, the magic, the awe will follow that letting go.

Anytime you try to dictate the how of manifestation, you limit the ingenuity of Infinite Intelligence to your own conscious limits of "this is how it can happen". You separate yourself from the breathtaking, miraculous means of Creation and confine the path of fulfilment to your limited ideas of what's acceptable and possible. What's acceptable and possible to your conscious mind is conditional knowledge and conditional expectation. It is informed by a limited view of the world, of the outcome, and of what can come into play to bring the outcome into place. Trying to control how things unfold makes you rigid, resistant, and ultimately insecure in what can come to pass in your experience. It can also overwhelm your system as the physical mind simply can't hold that much detail all at once. When you think you know the way, you actually end up getting in your own way. It is by dissolving all of your ideas of "how" into the limitless ocean of creativity that you truly open up to the creative ocean of Consciousness to come through and flow you into the right connections, moments, and circumstances that all arise to support the realization of your success.

Letting go of how your success materializes also allows you to include the reality of your success in your present moment and in your current field of awareness. It then, in your own perception, becomes a continuity of Consciousness from "here" or where you are right now to "there" or where you want to be – rather than a separate disconnected happening. If you know you are already on the road to your success, then you are inclined to naturally be in an open state, in a state of letting go, where you are not trying to control how things happen or unfold.

Control or the need to control what's unfolding comes about only when you continue to exclude your desired end from your impressions or perceptions of "what is" in your current reality framework. Often times, when you desire something, the reason you begin to make an effort and strive toward it with tension and struggle is that you have categorized it in the column of "things that are not" or "what is not". Somewhere in your own mind you create the premise that this desired end doesn't exist or isn't formed yet. This exclusion you've created in your mind then puts you into a state of wanting to move this desired end into the column of things that are, things that exist, and through that perception and effort you try your hardest to make it a part of "what is" for your experience. You go into defensive or offensive mode, either moving yourself into justification and excuses, or force, control and manipulation. None of these strategies are necessary however if you start with surrendering the belief that your desired end was separate and apart from you. If you saw desires as the realization of what's already accomplished for you, how you approach them would and does change.

Letting go of these control tendencies born of the mindset of separation naturally moves you into a state of reception. Separation or the perception that you are separate and apart from your environment makes you develop strategies for obtaining fulfilment from the lens of self and not-self. Control, worry, insecurity, force, manipulation and the like are all valid strategies for the separate self. In order for the separate self to get what it wants, it has to "do things" to the desired object to make it conform or behave in a way where the needs of the separate self get met. These same learned strategies formed from a worldview of separation are then employed in your deliberate creation efforts. When applied to conscious or deliberate creation, these strategies only prove to create more tension and stress for you.

The best activity for the mind once you have recognized the reality of your fulfilment is to move yourself into a state of reception by letting go, by trusting, by surrendering your version of how things should happen, need to happen, have to happen, or must happen. Give up control. Give up force. Give up worry. Give up figuring it out. Give up the need to make it happen. Give up the need to suffocate the flow of manifestation. Give up clinging. Give up the anxiety. Give up all those learned internal strategies around how to go about getting what you want. And then hold yourself in the space of gratitude for the reality of your fulfilment. Live in that space between gratitude and surrender.

What's it like to let go of thinking you know the means and the way?

What's it like to let go of thinking you have to figure out the "how" of your desired end?

What's it like to fully and completely let go of trying to control how this desired end will manifest?

What's it like to fully and completely trust Infinite Intelligence, the Universe to deliver your outcome to you in the highest and best possible way?

What's it like to feel gratitude for the reality of your fulfilment here and now?

Now notice how that feels and notice how trying to figure out the means, the way, the "how" of the equation in your mind. You move into different states instantly based on where you are holding yourself in relation to the successful outcomes you desire. Surrender and gratitude bring about one quality of feeling and being, and trying to figure out how and trying to control how bring about a different quality of being and feeling. Notice the difference and make note of it.

Letting go, surrendering, and being grateful for what's already accomplished in the unseen portions of your reality field do much more to support the fluid manifestation of your desired end than exercising the conscious mind in trying to figure out or control how it will appear to come to pass. Leave the how of manifestation to the Intelligence of Creation and let It hand it to you out of harmonious means and effortless flow. Effortless creation, effortless manifestation, effortless magnetism all emerge when you move yourself into states of surrender and gratitude after setting your intention and assuming the space of your fulfilment.

Conscious control and personal will create tension and friction because you are operating and moving from a more constricted awareness of all that is involved in the flow of manifestation. There's always so much more at work than your conscious mind can register, calculate, or discern. There are so many more intricate threads and synchronistic waves working behind the curtains of your sensory awareness. You do not have conscious awareness of all the cooperative components of your fulfilled end, your desired outcome. You don't consciously know what is in harmony, what is congruent, what path is the path of easy fulfilment. All of these aspects of manifestation are hidden to the limited abilities of conscious and selective awareness. And so it is more useful to let go, to trust, to dissolve the tension of figuring things out, to this greater deeper hidden movement of Creation.

Let yourself go

Deep into the Flow

Let what you think you know

Be dissolved in all that you don't know

As the Universe is a single harmonious system, a unified expanse of spiralling patterns and information, there is nothing to beat or bump against – everything is one flow, one movement.

There's nothing to do but let go.

Return to Now

Begin with the recognition that linear time is the sole child of the brain's processing capacity and that time is actually linear, simultaneous and non-existent all at once. This means, the past, present, and future, are as much parallel data streams streaming concurrently as they are sequential movements of events, and yet on another level of awareness they don't exist at all. In this model, the past is both in the past and is and isn't happening right now. The present is and is not happening right now. The future both hasn't happened yet and is and isn't happening right now. Within this model, there is no going or coming in any discreet way – coming of events and the going of events, the existence of them and the non-existence of them, their movement and motionlessness is simultaneous.

If you are completely focused in the illusion of linear continuity, the notion that the Now is all there is, is beyond the grasp of the well-rehearsed information processing you are accustomed to, focused in and looking out through. It is in the Now that all apparent coming and going seems to arise so before you can take advantage of what this Now-Space offers you, the access it gives you to both linear continuity and temporal simultaneity, you want to collect yourself completely into this pure point of creative power. There is a part of you that can experience and begin to utilize the simultaneous nature of time alongside the experience of linear continuity. And you want to leverage that.

One of the tendencies of moving into conscious creation is the relentless flight of the mind and attention into the desired end that the mind creates is "somewhere over there". You think about it. You picture it. You wonder about it. You are constantly engaged in mind activity on this "not here yet" experience. You project its existence into some future moment and then live your moments in relationship to that projection. You put it in front of you instead of putting yourself in that desired end right here and now. You want to look at this tendency. There is creative power in engaging the mind, in allowing the imagery of the desired end to flow, in allowing yourself to be immersed in the feeling space of your fulfilment.

There needs to be a balance between that ongoing inner activity which expends energy and your awareness of the only point of fulfilment in space-time – the Now. Being in the Now fully and completely gives you access to boundless flow, pure focus and expansive attention. It is a rejuvenating space of awareness that washes and melts away all the tension the ongoing inner activity that physical focus creates, while at the same time making available to you all the information you need to make the next moment your highest and best. Accessing the Now, being in the Now, dropping into the Heart, are all pointers to the only place and point of power in this Intelligent Universe. This hidden point of intersection between the space of Here and the time of Now, is the same as the middle point or line between the known and Unknown, the physical and the nonphysical, the material and nonmaterial, the actual and the potential. It is a powerful point of focus, of presence, and of being that gives you access to dimensions beyond time and space. You don't create in the future and you don't create in the past. These are all spaces or locations in the Field that you have access to right Now. The point of emergence, the point of manifestation, the point of fulfilment is all one, and that point is the Now. It is an entry point, a gateway or portal that allows you to impact, influence and reorganize space-time in all directions.

Sensory perception creates the illusion that this Now Space is about what appears right now. It is not. What appears right now is like a silhouette that's cast on a wall. It is superficial. The Space of the Now is a deep Ocean of Stillness – this is how your mind translates it, as an unmoving quietness, a place of total rest for the mind. This apparent absence of inactivity is only so because of what the mind mechanism is capable of translating. Your conscious mind can register a specific range of motion, frequency, velocity – beyond that range, it cannot perceive. That doesn't mean there is nothing there to perceive, it only appears that way. This space of apparent Stillness is the most powerful state you can bring yourself into. It is the fuel and fire of all of Creation and so allowing yourself to come back into it and maintain yourself in the resonance of it does much more to support the materialization of your desired end than keeping yourself in the mind realms of endless activity.

Forget about all of what appears right now and pay attention to the space that contains it. Feel the container of the contents of your now-moment, this is the Now and this is the place of flexibility, infinite potential, flow, surrender. Releasing what you think appears right now and dissolving all that you hold as yourself and as your present reality in the space of what appears, connects you to the unseen forces and resourceful dimensions of this Creative Universe. And that is exactly the space you want to bring yourself back into as frequently as the mind wants to take you into imagined future moments that it holds aren't here right now.

Nothing came before this Moment.

Nothing comes after this Moment.

The only place is Here.

The only time is Now.

You can say that there is a difference between "here" and "Here". This moment, the content of it is where you've never been. It is the ever-new kaleidoscope of patterns in which you find you're at the center of. Although it appears known, familiar, it is neither known nor familiar. This moment is a never-ending cascade of infinite possibilities blinking in and out of being. The contents of waking reality are made and remade numberless times. The newness of this moment is irrefutable, regardless of how it appears to the physical senses and to the mind that normalizes all new information into familiar patterns. You've never been in this unrepeatable moment, and you will never be in it again. This is the dance of ever-changing light.

And the other "Here", in the simplest terms, is where You reside always. You hold the best seat before the grand universal movie screen of waking life. Here there is no yesterday, no tomorrow, no today. This is your point of pure creative power, a motionless Space and a singular point in which nothing has ever happened and all is being created and recreated at the same time.

Everything is Here right Now. In the unified space of Creation, in the state of unity that underlies the diversity that appears all around you, everything already IS. Your fulfilment already IS in this space of Now. So giving your attention to this space, giving your awareness a break from desired content and into the space that already holds that content is a creative exercise in full on alignment and harmonization.

NOW is IT.

NOW is always IT.

There is no other time and there is no other place. There is no other point and there is no other space. NOW is it. You may not even be aware of how you've locked yourself into time-bound perception, in perception that is fragmenting experience into a linear format or framework and organizing all information into a "before, now, and after" format. It is the tendency of the mind to break up what is whole into chunks, parts, and time. The mind is an expert at exclusion, at "this is what is" and "this is what is not" so naturally you fall into projecting time frames in which what you perceive to not be here right now will be here later.

So it's a worthwhile exercise to check in with yourself, to check-in where you are holding yourself in relation to the Now. Are you consciously anchored in the immediacy, in the center, in the singularity of Being? Are you encoding reality from an inner space of pure presence? Or are you in the mental cycle of the past, the present and the future? Notice how it is that you fragment your experience into segments you label as past, present and future. Notice how it is that you organize information in temporal terms. Notice what emerges when you let all of these mental habits go and let yourself simply be present with nowhere to go, with nothing to move toward, and with nothing to put behind you. Noticing how you feel, how centered you feel, how present you feel, how anchored you feel will reveal to you where you are holding yourself in relation to the Now.

Any experience of tension is created when you leave yourself in the mind space of your being. Mind is activity, creative activity or destructive activity. Mind is motion and you will always know where you are locating yourself in your being by the level of ease, alertness, and energetic coherence you experience in the moment. If you are experiencing the present moment with clarity, feeling like all of your attention is here, all of your awareness is collected and clear, you are anchored in the Space of the Now. If you are experiencing tension, frustration, mental activity, uncertainty, any kind of motion, you are in the mind space and often in time-bound awareness.

There is no "there" to get to. There is no "going there" or "getting there" for there is only ever the Here and Now. Time and Space are created in the mind, and what you create in the mind will fill your experience of waking reality. NOW is It. NOW is always It.

It is the power of a unified perception, a singular awareness of unity, that allows all of your world and all that is in your world to come into the light of a greater order and harmony. When you are anchored in the Now, you are anchored in this unified state of wholeness. The mind of fragmentation, of separation, of diversity and multiplicity, creates the illusion that there are diverse and multiple unfolding's, conflicting plans even. Yet, when you are anchored and centered in the Now, you will see with clarity that there is only one stream, one field, one power, one plan unfolding itself as the manifested world. It is in your alignment with this seeing, with this unified perception, that you become a doorway to the miraculous and to the Infinite Possibilities of a great and intelligent design. It is in the unified perception the space of Now offers you that you access more of the creative power and current of Intelligence that forms all worlds.

Anchoring yourself in the Now is like turning on the Light. Clarity, restfulness, ease, peace, are all indicators of the free flow of energy through your being. It is only the Now that gives you access to this free flow. You want to always seek this anchor point first, always notice if you've turned the Light on before you move through the moments of your waking experience. The energy that enters and flows freely as you anchor yourself in the space of the Now is one that harmonizes, corrects, and adjusts whatever patterns of resistance you may have generated while dwelling in the mind-spaces of thought, thinking, and figuring things out.

What the conscious mind can't think of , what the conscious mind can't conceive of, all dwells in this expansive space of apparent Stillness. Aligning yourself to this space of Now-ness, anchoring your attention in this space and feeling of being fully present, is the magic formula of the creative process. It is in this apparent Stillness that all things exist and are accomplished. And resonating alongside it or with it ensures the effortless flow of your desired end. The NOW is It. The NOW is always IT.

Centered in the Now, you are unstoppable. Connected to the full flow and stream of pure Consciousness, pure creative force, you are irresistible to all that you desire to experience and more. Lao Tzu pointedly expressed that "to the mind that is Still, the whole Universe surrenders." The power and fuel of all fulfilment lives in this Now Space of being, in Being Here fully and completely. Half occupied by an imagined future, half absorbed by the idea that what you desire is elsewhere, you limit the flow of the Intelligence that is forming every part of the world.

There is no mental effort required or struggle to be engaged in. Everything already is right now. Everything already exists right now. When you balance the creative ventures of the mind with this anchored state of pure awareness, you access and make use of more than your personal will and power. It is your being anchored in the Now that connects you to the flow of a greater power, to the flow of greater forces beyond the boundaries of your personhood.

Give your full attention to this Now space. Recognize it for the powerful seat of creativity that it is. Now IS IT. NOW is always It.

More to You Than Meets the Eyes

The greater part of your awareness is beyond the conscious mind. The possibilities, forces, and functions of your conscious mind are only a small fraction of what the larger unseen portions of your being are capable of. You are a unified whole, greater and beyond measure than your fragmenting everyday awareness can allow you to realize. Surface awareness, sensory awareness, is superficial, only registering a small spectrum of the flux of information that is available. There is always more to be accessed, perceived, tuned into, and attuned to.

What you observe yourself doing in your state of wakefulness is a very minute or minuscule fragment of the vast unseen activity you are engaging in and being engaged by. What determines and decides, the propelling force of your being is always in what appears as the invisible spheres of your whole being – it is the unseen aspects of you that drive you. There is always more of you than can consciously be observed, registered, processed – tap into this. For it is this that will allow you and afford you the recognition that everything, every possible thing, is within your reach. And that absolutely nothing can ever be in your way.

If you were to right now tune into the greater unseen aspects of your being if you were to right now expand your conscious awareness and feel into your broader wholeness, what shifts for you and from where does it shift?

If just for right now you were to recognize that you are immensely greater than all that you are aware of being in this moment, what changes?

The field of Consciousness you think and act from in your everyday waking state is reflected in the content of thought and action you play out. This is what lets you know how small or wide a line you have drawn in the parameters of the self you express. There is always a greater field to source from, a greater field of awareness, of thought, of self-reference. In an infinite pool of creative life, there is no end to the lines of inclusively you create in what and how you understand yourself, in what and who you know yourself to be. The more you contemplate your true parameters of being, the more you create a template of Consciousness around limitlessness, the more you expand the possibilities of your expression, demonstrations, and overall experience of living. Mediocrity is the story of a limited self, the illusory projection of Consciousness that maintains itself as limited, separate, and independent of the vast Field of Creative Intelligence that is the source and cause of all.

What exactly is within reach for a being without boundaries and limitations?

When you recognize that even your biggest dreams are within reach, that you are more than equal to your highest dreams, all apparent barriers, perceptions of "things" that are in the way disappear. First, they disappear from within your own psyche, within your own field of perception. It is as you realize that there is no thought, feeling, expectation, or event that can actually deter, thwart or distract you from those things you want to experience, that those apparent obstacles disappear on the external stage of waking reality. Nothing is actually out of reach. Everything is actually accessible, reachable, touchable, and grasp-able. You have universal access. It is all your own body. You have cosmic access. It is all your own unified nature. There is no end to the heights of success you can reach no matter how you define or have defined that success. There is no cap. There is no ceiling. For as long as you grow or expand yourself to these fields, you will demonstrate the content of those fields in your own unique way.

The apparent limitations of the personality you make use of can change as you move into a different field of resonance. As you change the circumference of your perceptual sphere, what you access, what you relate to, and what you ultimately materialize also changes. With awareness and exercise of self-change, latent tendencies or dormant tendencies can become active. With this activation, a new pattern of self is brought to the surface and into expression. This is all you are doing. You are reaching deep into your limitless being to activate and bring into being new possibilities of self, new patterns of being. It is this evolution of self, this rebirth of your own being and point of reference into new fields of resonance that externalizes as new experiences that tell your story of never-ending greatness.

Enormous power and innumerable possibilities already bubble deep within the heart of every being. To summon your greatness, to actualize yourself into your own desired success is a reality and capacity contained within the very technology of your embodiment and expression in human form. You will always be more than you appear to be. With this recognition in your awareness, with this realization placed at the forefront of your conscious awareness, you can always look to the vast hidden resources inside yourself, and vast they are and vast they will always remain. There will always be more to you and more of you to be expressed, extended, made visible.

Let your mantra be: There is an immensity inside of me coming into expression. There is so much

NOTHING IN THE WAY

of me in the unseen, unknown portions of reality that I can always draw from.

Have you consciously considered the powers and possibilities within you?

How can you express the immensity of your being into your desired success?

There always has been, there is, and always will be so much more to you than meets the eyes.

You are the exaltation of all life.

The limitless in me bows to the limitless in you.

Nothing is in your way.

KIDEST OM

Author's Note

Dear Reader,

I want to thank you for reading. I hope the ideas and guidance in this book helped you to access or reaffirm the wisdom and understanding already within you. My intention with all my work is that it helps, supports and reinforces your knowing of your power and reminds you of just how cosmically blessed, connected, eternally empowered and loved you are. The basis of all that we are is a love that is powerful and a power that is loving.

If you enjoyed this book and have a minute to spare, I would appreciate a review on Amazon from you. Reviews from readers like you can help new readers connect to my work to find the help, support and reinforcement they need in their own empowerment and transformation journey.

Thank you again for joining me in catching up to our collective expansion.

Infinite Blessings to you in all that you are and all that you do.

With great love and gratitude,
Kidest OM
http://infinite-life.com

P.S. If you'd like to receive ongoing reminders on your power and potential, you can connect to my social media channels under @KidestOm. I update them regularly with reminders, new insights and more tools, tips and guidance.

About Kidest Om

Kidest OM is the author of several books and publications on the power and primacy of Consciousness. With a degree in Psychology and a decade of studying various disciplines on the nature of reality, Kidest writes and speaks exclusively on self-mastery and reality engineering.

She has created numerous informative audios and videos on these subjects reaching thousands of viewers and listeners worldwide. Kidest also consults with clients from all over the world through her private coaching and consultation practice.

An avid reader, meditator and lover of nature Kidest currently lives in the Pacific North West and describes life in the West Coast as the perfect backdrop for conversations on the evolutionary potential inherent in all beings everywhere.

For information regarding books and programs by Kidest or her private practice, please visit http://infinite-life.com